Listening/Speaking
Strategies and Activities

Mary Shepard Wong

You said it!

Listening/Speaking Strategies and Activities

CAMBRIDGE
UNIVERSITY PRESS

PUBLISHED BY THE PRESS SYNDICATE OF THE UNIVERSITY OF CAMBRIDGE
The Pitt Building, Trumpington Street, Cambridge, United Kingdom

CAMBRIDGE UNIVERSITY PRESS
The Edinburgh Building, Cambridge CB2 2RU, UK   http://www.cup.cam.ac.uk
40 West 20th Street, New York, NY 10011–4211, USA   http://www.cup.org
10 Stamford Road, Oakleigh, Melbourne 3166, Australia
Ruiz de Alarcón 13, 28014 Madrid, Spain

First published by St. Martin's Press, Inc. 1998

Second printing 2000

Printed in the United States of America

Library of Congress Cataloging-in-Publication Data Available

ISBN 0 521 65786 5 Student's Book
ISBN 0 521 65785 7 Instructor's Manual
ISBN 0 521 65805 5 Audiocassettes

Cover photograph © David Oliver / Tony Stone Images

To

Laura, my favorite ice skater in all the world;

Justin, my little bundle who came into being

at the same time as this book;

Sam, my husband and friend;

And Mom and Dad, my ever-faithful cheering section.

I love you all.

Contents

▶ **CHAPTER 5   CONDUCTING AN INTERVIEW**
   Eiko: This Strange Country!

HELP WITH VOCABULARY   72

PART I: FOCUS ON LISTENING — Eiko: This Strange Country!   73

Eiko lives with an English-speaking family in the United States and is grateful for the chance to speak English every day, but she finds some of their ways strange. Students listen as Eiko reads her journal entry, and then they are asked to make suggestions for new foreign students in the United States. Later, Eiko completes a graph reflecting her adjustment process, and students do the same.

PART II: FOCUS ON SPEAKING — Conducting an Interview   79

Students consider topics, questions, and strategies for the interviews they will do.

USEFUL EXPRESSIONS: EXPRESSIONS USED TO INTERRUPT, TO ASK FOR REPETITION, AND TO GET FEEDBACK 82

▶ **CHAPTER 6   GIVING AN IMPROMPTU SPEECH**
               Thien: Homesick and Sick of English   *97*

HELP WITH VOCABULARY 98

PART I: FOCUS ON LISTENING — Thien: Homesick and Sick of English 99

Thien is not adjusting very well to life in the United States. When he is outside the classroom, he speaks, reads, and listens to Vietnamese instead of English. He has gotten low grades on most of his projects, but he does not want to drop the class. Students listen as Thien's teacher speaks with him.

Pre-Listening Task: *Predicting Causes and Solutions*
                   for Thien's Poor Grades 99

🔲 **Listening Task:** *Listening for the Main Ideas of the Dialogue* 100

Post-Listening Task: *Role-Playing a Teacher-Student Dialogue* 100

PART II: FOCUS ON SPEAKING — Giving an Impromptu Speech 101

Thien delivers an impromptu speech about gun control. Having had a friend shot by a stray bullet one New Year's Eve, Thien feels strongly about the issue. After organizing his thoughts, he volunteers to speak up and he presents his points in a coherent and moving short speech for which he receives an *A*. Students discuss the important elements of a good presentation.

Pre-Speaking Task 1: *Discussing the Dos and Don'ts of Delivering a Speech* 101

🔲 **Pre-Speaking Task 2:** *Listening to a Sample Impromptu Speech* 101

To the Teacher

▶ **INTRODUCTION**

You Said It! Listening/Speaking Strategies and Activities is an intermediate listening/speaking text developed to empower ESL students preparing for their careers and/or college in an English-speaking environment. The text is designed for students who want to improve their English fluency and accuracy in order to achieve academic, career, social, and personal goals. It is unique in that it provides not only step-by-step instructions for ten student-centered projects but also models for those projects. These models, or sample projects, are presented by four fictitious ESL students in the text. The stories of these "textbook peers"— how they struggle with the speaking projects in their ESL class and with adjusting to a new culture — provide a relevant, ongoing story line that integrates the listening and speaking sections in the text.

Organization

Each chapter introduces a specific problem that one textbook peer is having in his or her cultural adjustment. For example: Abdul has problems with discrimination at work; Eiko has difficulties with her homestay American family; Thien cannot find friends or situations in which to speak English; Maria feels she is too old and has too many responsibilities to continue her studies.

Students learn about these problems in each chapter's *Part I: Focus on Listening* section. They listen to the textbook peers present a monologue, a dialogue, or the speaking project itself. They respond by discussing the problems of the textbook peer and posing possible solutions. Each listening segment has a series of tasks in the pre-listening, listening, and post-listening phases. Guessing, predicting, listing, small-group discussions, and recalling are pre-listening tasks. Finding the main idea, listening for specific information, note taking, and filling in are some of the tasks done during listening. Post-listening tasks include small-group work, role play, and critical thinking aimed at offering suggestions and solutions to problems.

Each chapter also introduces a speaking project that the textbook peers model in *Part II: Focus on Speaking*. For example, for the project in which students are asked to record a 5- to 10-minute self-introduction, students first listen to and take notes about the recorded mini-lecture that describes the assignment. Then students listen to and evaluate the monologue tapes made by the four textbook peers: Abdul, Eiko, Maria, and Thien. After evaluating these tapes by the same criteria that their own tapes will be evaluated, students are well prepared to record their self-introductions. This section of each chapter focuses on speaking and has a series of tasks much like those in the listening section. There are pre-speaking tasks to prepare students for the speaking projects, the speaking projects themselves, and post-speaking tasks to bring closure to the projects.

▶ RATIONALE

Given enough motivation, opportunity, and guidance, students will become active participants in the learning process. Students will be motivated by discussing the problems of students much like themselves. Students are given opportunities to take an active role in learning by selecting the focus and content of their projects (which include surveys, movie reviews, interviews, impromptu speeches, prepared speeches, debates, commercials, and cultural events). They are given enough guidance and support to accomplish each project by means of the explanations, exercises, and examples in the text and by two boxes found in each chapter. The "Help with Vocabulary" boxes introduce vocabulary in context that might be new to students, and the "Useful Expressions" boxes highlight expressions needed in the listening and/or speaking tasks. There are also two vocabulary review sections following Chapters 5 and 10; in these, students fill in the correct vocabulary word in the context of a story, a dialogue, or some other real-life situation.

Approach

You Said It! is different from other ESL textbooks in that students are not asked merely to complete rote exercises after listening to unrelated, isolated segments of dialogue; nor are instructors expected to plan and orchestrate projects tacked on to the end of a chapter under the title "follow-up activities." Instead, students are involved in an ongoing story line, and they participate in ten classroom-tested, learner-centered speaking projects which require communication with others in and outside the classroom. The text is written with an awareness of the whole person; it helps the students through the process of cultural adjustment, asking them to consider solutions to problems they may experience academically, professionally, socially, or personally. The supportive tone and cooperative approach within the text help students learn, and make them aware that they are not alone in their endeavor to accomplish their goals. The instructor is a facilitator, empowering the learners by creating a nurturing environment and providing a range of learning strategies. Students explore a variety of strategies that enable them to get over the fear of speaking up in class, striking up conversations with native English speakers, and conducting interviews. These strategies help students whose learning styles range from introverted to extroverted, from analytical to impulsive, to learn from one another.

The text is developed with an awareness of the importance of integrating the four skills (listening, speaking, reading, and writing). Multi-skill learning can have a greater impact than single-skill work because of the reinforcement that the skills have on one another. Yet the text focuses on listening and speaking in order to fit into more traditional ESL classes that are labeled according to skill area. The text provides the opportunity for authentic, meaningful communication as students are asked to accomplish tasks that interest them. The text also prods students to become learners of culture so that they may become bicultural as well as bilingual. Both the target culture and the cultures of classmates are explored so that an understanding and acceptance of cultural differences can be developed.

The cassettes that accompany the text are designed for in-class use by the instructor. The Tapescript as well as the Answer Key are in the text itself for easy reference. Note that some pages containing various forms are intended for students to tear out and turn in. An Instructor's Manual is available, which has time estimates, suggestions, additional activities and ideas for adapting the text for use in an EFL setting. It also offers a complete tapescript.

▶ PLANNING THE SEMESTER

There is enough material in the text for over sixty hours of class instruction, but the text can easily be expanded or shortened. The text can be expanded by allowing more time for speaking tasks, adding pronunciation lessons when appropriate, and doing the extra activities suggested in the Instructor's Manual. However, most instructors run out of semester before running out of text, so it is wise to first examine the projects and time estimates of each chapter, consider the needs of your students, and then decide which chapters students would enjoy and benefit from the most.

Although the amount of time needed to spend on the various tasks, activities, and projects varies with each instructor and class, knowing approximately how long they take helps in preparing lesson plans. The following time estimates are intended as a guide or rule of thumb to give you flexibility and freedom to expand, shorten, or even leave out various tasks, activities, projects, or chapters. They assume that there are thirty to thirty-five students in the class, that nothing goes wrong, and that you keep things moving at a fast pace. Be sure to factor in to each day the time needed for taking attendance, making announcements, teaching pronunciation, taking breaks, and so forth. (A more detailed breakdown of time estimates appears in the Instructor's Manual.)

	Chapter	In-Class Time Estimate	Homework Time Estimate
1.	Contract	3 hr, 30 min	30 min
2.	Monologue Tape	4 hr	2 hr, 30 min
3.	Group Survey	7 hr, 30 min	3 hr, 30 min
4.	Movie Review	4 hr	3 hr, 30 min
5.	Personal Interview	4 hr	3 hr, 30 min
6.	Impromptu Speech	5 hr	2 hr, 30 min
7.	Prepared Speech	9 hr	6 hr, 30 min
8.	Debates	8 hr, 30 min	3 hr, 30 min
9.	Commercial	4 hr, 30 min	1 hr
10.	Cultural Summary and Culture Booths	10 hr	3 hr
	Total:	**60 hr**	**30 hr**

One way to reduce the amount of material is to skip chapters. Which chapters to skip depends on the specific needs of your students. Chapters 3, 7, and 8 (the survey, the prepared speech, and the debate) are the most challenging and academic. Chapters 4, 5, and 9 (the movie review, the interview, and the commercial) are easier and less academic. Chapters 1 and 10 give an introduction and conclusion to the text, and so it is recommended to include them. The monologue tape in Chapter 2 is a great assignment in that it doesn't take up much class time and yet gives students practice communicating their ideas; it also gives you a chance to get to know them. Chapter 6, the impromptu speech, is recommended because it builds confidence for the prepared speech in Chapter 7. If you plan to skip Chapter 7, Chapter 6 is still recommended because it gives students the experience of giving at least a short speech. Another alternative is to include all the chapters but to skip the listening tasks that don't directly model the speaking projects and to skip any speaking tasks that are not necessary to prepare the students for the major speaking assignments.

▶ GRADING

Students usually like to know up front the weight of each assignment and how it will be graded. The following assignment/progress sheet (which can be modified to reflect your specific assignments, grading requirements, and scheduling) may prove useful. (More specific suggestions about how to grade each project are given in the Instructor's Manual.)

Percent of Grade	Project	Chapter and Due Date	Total Points Possible	My Total Points
10%	Monologue Tape	Ch. 2: Due _____	100 points	_____
10%	Survey/Report	Ch. 3: Due _____	100 points	_____
10%	Movie Review	Ch. 4: Due _____	100 points	_____
10%	Interview	Ch. 5: Due _____	100 points	_____
10%	Impromptu Speech	Ch. 6: Due _____	100 points	_____
10%	Prepared Speech	Ch. 7: Due _____	100 points	_____
10%	Debate	Ch. 8: Due _____	100 points	_____
10%	Video Commercial	Ch. 9: Due _____	100 points	_____
10%	Summary Exercise	Ch. 10: Due _____	100 points	_____
10%	Culture Booth	Ch. 10: Due _____	100 points	_____

▶ ORGANIZATION OF THE TEXT

The Opening Illustration

Each chapter begins with an opening illustration of the character or characters featured in the chapter. A caption and/or question is used to get students thinking about the content of the listening tasks to follow. Ask students to look at the illustration, describe what is going on, read the caption, and answer the questions. After students have discussed the opening illustration, proceed to "Help with Vocabulary."

"Help with Vocabulary" Box

Following the illustration is the "Help with Vocabulary" box. It introduces words used in the chapter that may be new to some students. All the vocabulary words appear in bold type the first time they are used in the text or the Answer Key. The words are presented in the context of a sentence chosen to help students guess the meaning. For variety, three different formats are used for vocabulary exercises, all requiring only 10 to 20 minutes to complete. The first format is used in Chapters 1, 5, and 8. It requires students to listen to the word as used in a sentence, guess its meaning and part of speech from context, discuss the guesses as a class, and then match the definitions with the words. Students are asked to guess the meaning of words in context before matching them to definitions so that they will acquire the skill of learning vocabulary from context rather than from a dictionary. A review of the parts of speech and their abbreviations might be helpful in the first chapter. The second vocabulary exercise format is found in Chapters 2, 4, 7, and 10. Students first read the word in the context of a sentence and then match the definition. If time is tight, you can ask students to do these exercises for homework the day before they begin the chapter in class. Then the vocabulary can be discussed quickly. The final vocabulary exercise format is used in Chapters 3, 6, and 9. It asks students to first match the definitions and words and then to fill in the words in the context of sentences. The words in the vocabulary boxes appear in the order they are seen in the text or heard on the tape; however, they have been scrambled in Chapters 1 and 4, so students will not simply copy them in order when doing the cloze activities.

Part I: Focus on Listening

Each chapter has two main sections: *Part I: Focus on Listening;* and *Part II: Focus on Speaking.* Part I has a variety of pre-listening, listening, and post-listening tasks.

Cartoons

Cartoons help to introduce or reinforce a point made in the text or some aspect of life in the United States. Students should look at the cartoon carefully, read the caption, and try to catch the humor. It often helps if you read the cartoon with a lot of expression to help students get the joke. The questions and comments about the cartoons are meant to focus attention on the point in the text that the cartoons relate to.

Pre-Listening Tasks

As stated earlier, guessing, predicting, listing, recalling, and small-group work are pre-listening tasks. Their purpose is to prepare students for the listening tasks that follow. Follow the step-by-step instructions of each task.

Small-Group Work Procedures

The class can form small groups in various ways. You can ask students to group themselves or can group them each time or can use some specific criterion (such as forming groups of three in which at least one member speaks a different language or has lived in the United States for more than two years — or is married, or is working, and so on). After groups are formed, students exchange first names and select a leader. Students take turns being leaders. The leader's job is to encourage quiet students to speak up, to make sure everyone in the group is given a chance to speak, and to see that the group stays on task, following the steps clearly spelled out in the text. You can walk from group to group answering any questions and making sure that all groups remain on task.

"Useful Expressions" Box

Within the first pre-listening task or at some other point, students are asked to refer to the "Useful Expressions" box. The purpose of this box is to give students guidance to accomplish the task at hand; it provides grammatical phrases and helps them avoid reinforcing grammatical errors. You can discuss the content of the box as a class directly before it is needed for the task, or students can use it individually for reference; however, the focus of the class should remain on communicating and fluency rather than on accuracy or repeating grammatically correct sentences.

Listening Tasks

Listening tasks include finding the main idea, listening for specific information, note taking, evaluating, and filling in. The cassette tapes provide the listening component of the text and are designed to be used in class. Some of the listening tasks can be skipped, but be sure to include tasks that provide a model for the speaking projects in Part II of the chapter.

Post-Listening Tasks

Post-listening tasks include small-group discussions, critical thinking, and role-playing, among others. These activities bring closure to the listening section by having students reflect about what they have learned.

Part II: Focus on Speaking

Part II of each chapter centers on a speaking project. Like Part I, it offers activities that prepare students (pre-speaking tasks), along with specific projects (speaking tasks) and activities to bring closure to the projects (post-speaking tasks).

Pre-Speaking Tasks

The pre-speaking tasks are designed to help students prepare for the speaking tasks. For example, when the speaking project involves finding English speakers to talk with, such as in conducting a survey or interview, this section offers strategies for finding and approaching willing subjects. In addition to role-playing, other pre-speaking tasks ask students to evaluate the speaking tasks completed by the four textbook peers.

Speaking Tasks

These tasks are the core of the speaking section of each chapter, and it is essential that students prepare for and participate in the speaking tasks. They include the monologue tape, survey and report, movie review and report, interview, impromptu speech, prepared speech, debate, commercial, explanation and summary, and culture booths.

Post-Speaking Tasks

Post-speaking tasks are used as a wrap-up activity and as an assessment of the speaking project. For example, students may watch a videotape of their own speech and write an evaluation.

Vocabulary Review Sections

There are two vocabulary review sections, following Chapter 5 and Chapter 10. Vocabulary words from each chapter are reviewed separately to make it convenient if some chapters were skipped. Each chapter's review is a complete story in itself, so students again are using vocabulary in context, but this time in a different context from the chapter. The vocabulary reviews can be used as class exercises, quizzes, or homework. They can be done one at a time, immediately following each chapter, or as a comprehensive review and a means to check up at the middle and the end of the course. They are designed so these pages can be torn out and collected.

ACKNOWLEDGMENTS

The number of people who contribute to the development of a book that is attributed to one author is staggering. In my case it ranges from the person in the audience at my first TESOL presentation in 1992 who asked for the name of my book (whoever you are, you made me believe that my ideas were worthy of publication) to the board of St. Martin's Press that decided to take on the project, and to the many people in between who helped transform an enthusiastic teacher into a published author.

I would like to thank the people at St. Martin's Press: Naomi Silverman, my acquisitions editor, who believed in the "novel idea" of the project, specifically the story line of textbook peers; and Carl Whithaus, the associate editor at the beginning of the project. Tina Carver, the sponsoring editor was instrumental to the project, lending her expertise at crucial stages of development — as was Kimberly Wurtzel, the assistant editor. I would also like to thank Emily Berleth, Manager of Publishing Services, for showing great patience and perseverance in working through the many details of production. I am indebted to Tünde A. Dewey for skillfully transforming the manuscript into an attractive text, and to Anna Veltfort for the graphics that make the characters come alive on the pages.

I wish to express my further gratitude to the reviewers for St. Martin's Press, whose comments and insights helped select the contents of the chapters.

Rebecca Freeman, University of Pennsylvania; Stacy Hagen, Edmonds Community College; Helen Heck, Rider University; Lillian Kutz, University of Illinois at Urbana-Champaign; Alan D. Lytle, University of Southern Mississippi; Kevin McClure, ESL Language Centers-San Francisco; Judith Lynn Paiva, Northern Virginia Community College; Valerie Pierce, Butler University; Nadia F. Scholnick, City College of San Francisco; Doug Woken, Sangamon State University.

To Tom Lew, my dean at El Camino College, I give thanks for encouraging me in the area of professional development, funding attendance at conferences, allowing flexible scheduling for graduate research relating to teaching and the development of classroom materials, and ever-present support and confidence in my abilities. Finally, I would like to acknowledge the support of my colleagues at El Camino College, and thank all my ESL students whose useful comments helped me revise the tasks and activities in the text.

The contract of the book coincided with the birth of my second child, and its completion came with my acceptance to graduate school; so it is obvious that this working/studying mom had a support system at home that needs some applause. To my mother-in-law, who breaks all the stereotypes, thank you for watching Justin while I was at work, and for being the ultimate Chinese-language teacher for myself and my children. To my in-laws, Jan and Larry, my heartfelt appreciation for helping with the kids on the weekends when I needed extra time to work. Laura, thanks for watching JT; and Sam, thanks for putting up with it all. Lastly, I wish to thank my mother and father for their loving support and encouragement.

CHAPTER 1

Making a Contract to Improve My English

▶ ABDUL, EIKO, MARIA, AND THIEN: ANXIOUS THOUGHTS

Abdul, Eiko, Maria, and Thien, four ESL students, are **anxious*** as they wait in the registration line. What do you think they might be thinking about?

*Note: Words in **bold** type are defined in each chapter's "Help with Vocabulary" box. They also appear in the Glossary at the back of the book. They are bold only the first time they appear in the text or Tapescript, which is in the Answer Key.

Help with Vocabulary

Cover up the definitions at the bottom of this box. As you listen to the instructor read each sentence, guess the *meaning* of the **bold** word and its *part of speech* (verb, noun, adjective, adverb, preposition, or idiom). After each sentence, discuss which context clues helped you make your guess.

1. Before I take tests, I get **anxious** and bite my nails.
2. Let me **jot down** your phone number in my address book.
3. It can **frustrate** me when I know what to say but I can't say it in English.
4. I should **keep track of** all the money I spend by eating out.
5. His dream is not to work for anyone and to become an **entrepreneur.**
6. His parents are very **strict.** He cannot go out on weeknights.
7. She may **chicken out** and not take the class with the strict instructor.
8. I work the night **shift** and don't get home until 6 A.M.
9. He got straight *A*'s in high school, a perfect 4.0 **GPA.**
10. Because of her poor grades, she is on academic **probation.**
11. It is hard to **get** the baby **down for a nap** with the TV on.
12. When I get **embarrassed,** my cheeks turn bright red.
13. My boss is too **demanding.** I can never please him.
14. Working three part-time jobs is **suicide!** Don't work so hard.

Write the correct number of the sentence above that the **bold** word is in next to the definition. Then, write the word and indicate its part of speech (verb (v.), noun (n.), adjective (adj.), adverb (adv.), preposition (prep.), or idiom). Follow the example.

____ a. the grade-point average of all one's grades _____

____ b. a person who organizes and manages a business _____

____ c. ashamed, humiliated _____

____ d. to disappoint _____

____ e. a period of testing that will determine one's outcome _____

____ f. a period of time at work _____

1 g. worried, afraid   *anxious (adj.)*

____ h. to kill oneself, or if used idiomatically, to do something difficult or dangerous intentionally _____

____ i. to write down quickly _____

____ j. to try to get a child to sleep a short time during the day _____

____ k. requiring a lot of _____

____ l. enforces rules severely _____

____ m. to keep a record of, to remember _____

____ n. to not do something because one is afraid _____

Correct your answers by discussing them or by checking the Answer Key.

PART I: FOCUS ON LISTENING

Abdul, Eiko, Maria, and Thien: Anxious Thoughts

Mrs. Mutner liked to go over a few of her rules on the first day of school.

- Why are the students shocked?
- What do you think of some of the teacher's rules?
- Which ones are funny?
- Have you ever felt the way these students feel on your first day of school?

▶ PRE-LISTENING TASK

A. Working in groups of three, exchange first names within your group. Then discuss the following questions. (Refer to the "Useful Expressions" box at the end of this chapter for help in forming the sentences needed for this activity.)

1. What do you remember about your first day of school as a child?
2. On that day, what did you look forward to and what were you anxious about?
3. What childhood school experience scared you the most?
4. In this class, what are you looking forward to or anxious about?
5. What do you think your classmates are looking forward to or anxious about?

B. As a group, complete the following lists of things that students might be anxious about or might look forward to.

Things That May Make Students Anxious

giving a speech _____ _____

_____ _____ _____

_____ _____ _____

Things That Students May Look Forward To

meeting new friends _____ _____

_____ _____ _____

_____ _____ _____

C. Choose one person from your group who will report to the class what you have discussed.

▶ LISTENING TASK 1

A. One way to improve your listening is to use a *listening strategy* that involves listening for a specific purpose. In this exercise your purpose is to listen for the *main idea*. Listen to the thoughts of four students in the registration line, and **jot down** their main ideas in note form as shown for Student 1. What is each student anxious about? Do not try to write down every word they say.

Student 1 — *Abdul*

the long line, getting in the class, staying in the classes

_____

_____

Student 2 — *Eiko*

_____

_____

_____

Student 3 — *Maria*

_____

_____

_____

Student 4 — *Thien*

_____

_____

_____

B. Discuss your answers for Step A with the entire class.

▶ LISTENING TASK 2

A. This time, listen for the important, *stressed* words that each student says. Fill in the blanks when you hear a pause. You have studied some of these words in the "Help with Vocabulary" box.

ABDUL: What a line! Even if I do get all my _____ 1 , I don't know if I

will be able to stay in them if my _____ 2 schedule changes.

Working _____ 3 hours a week and taking 12 units is

_____ 4 . What if I can't keep up with the homework or I'm

asked to work _____ 5 at work? I hope I get an easy teacher. I

heard that Miller is _____ 6 and _____ 7 ,

making you do movie reviews, debates, and interviews and

_____ 8 your grade after only four absences. I hope Miller isn't

the only _____ 9 left by the time I register. This line better get

moving, or I'll be late for my afternoon _____ 10 . It was a lot

simpler back home. There, students don't have to work to _____ 11 .

EIKO: I hope I do _____ in my classes. If I don't get a high enough
1

_____, I will lose my chance to study here. Maybe Cindy,
2

the girl I live with in the United States, will _____ me with my
3

homework. She is always so _____ with her boyfriends
4

though. I bet _____ in the class has lived here for years
5

and speaks like a _____. I hope there will be some other
6

_____ students in the class. If I find out we have to do any
7

speeches, I'll _____ and take a reading class. Maybe I can
8

take a Japanese class; that would be an _____ A. Why didn't
9

I pay _____ in my English classes in elementary school in
10

Japan? What if I don't understand what the teacher says and am too

_____ to ask her to repeat? What if I _____
11   12

and am sent back to Japan without a _____? What time is it
13

in Japan now? I wonder what my _____ are doing.
14

MARIA: I am so _____! What am I doing here? I must be the
1

_____ one in line. Some of these _____
2   3

look as though they should be in junior high school. Maybe the classes are

already _____, and I won't be able to get in. I probably
4

can't _____ it anyway. Someone said that the
5

_____ went up again. That can't be true. They went
6

up last semester. I wonder what the _____ will cost. I
7

hope the kids are OK at my brother's house. He'll never get José

_____ with all those other kids there. Maybe I will
8

have time to pick up some meat for _____ before I pick
9

them up. By the looks of this line, I'll be here for dinner. Oh my. I have so many

things to _____ about, it is almost impossible to
10

_____ them all.
11

THIEN: I'm so _____ about my grades. I hope I get an easy teacher. I

1

can't fail this class again. Being on _____, if I fail, I'm out;

2

and then I'll never learn how to speak English. I can't get a _____

3

if I can't speak English. Sometimes I _____ English. I'll never

4

be able to speak and understand it as I do _____. Maybe I'll

5

just live in Little Saigon and be a waiter speaking Vietnamese. A _____?

6

I came all this way to be a waiter? No. I want a better job. Yeah, I want to

_____ my own place, to be my own boss, an

7

_____. I'll have twenty guys working for me. Sure! That is,

8

if I ever get through this _____ line.

9

B. Correct your answers by discussing them or by checking the Answer Key.

▶ POST-LISTENING TASK

A. Form groups of three, and discuss the fears of one of these students: Abdul,
Eiko, Maria, or Thien. Write down what you might say to that student if he or she
were your friend.

_____

_____

_____

_____

_____

_____

_____

_____

B. Choose one person from your group who will report to the class what you have
discussed.

PART II: FOCUS ON SPEAKING

Making a Contract to Improve My English

▶ **PRE-SPEAKING TASK**

A. Thien does not have many situations in which he can speak English. In groups of three, think of different situations in which Thien could speak English. Write them in the spaces provided.

laundry room in your apartment building

_____

_____

_____

_____

_____

_____

_____

B. Choose one person from your group who will report to the class what you have discussed.

▶ **SPEAKING TASK 1**

A. As a class, read and discuss the contract on the opposite page.

B. Spend a few minutes to fill out the contract, and sign it.

C. With one other student in class, discuss what you have committed to do to improve your English. Then answer the following questions.

1. Why may it be difficult for you to fulfill this contract?
2. Why is the contract important?

D. Tell the class some ways you have found to listen to and speak more English.

E. After a few weeks, ask your partner about his or her success with the contract.

Some people study a foreign language for years and never really speak it. Others have spoken a foreign language for years without ever having studied it. Why is that? How does one really learn another language? Learning to speak a language is like learning to ride a bike or play a musical instrument. It takes a lot of practice and patience, not a lot of lectures.

How much out-of-class time do you spend actually listening to and speaking English? Can you do more to study English? How are you studying it? What might be some better ways to study — ways in which you both listen to and speak with people?

Fill in the following contract.

CONTRACT

At present

Outside of this class, I *listen to* English an average of _____ hours a day.

Outside of this class, I *speak* English an average of _____ hours a day.

Outside of this class, I *study* English by _____.

Starting this week

Outside of this class, I will try *to listen* to English an average

of _____ hours a day.

Outside of this class, I will try to *speak* English an average

of _____ hours a day.

Outside of this class, I will try to *study* English

by _____.

Name: _____

Date: _____

A. Find a partner who is a stranger to you. If possible, find someone who speaks a different language than you do. Prepare to introduce your partner to the class by exchanging personal information with him or her.

B. Use the information worksheet below to record your partner's information. (Do *not* write your *own* information.) Change the topics (numbers 1 to 7) on the worksheet into information questions. For example, for number 3, ask, "How long have you lived in the United States?" If you discover something you and your partner have in common, or something very interesting about your partner, write that down under numbers 8 and 9.

C. When it's your turn, stand up, and introduce your partner to the class. State his or her name clearly. Then tell the class a few interesting things about your partner, but do *not* tell everything you wrote on the worksheet. Begin your introduction by saying, "My name is _____, and I would like to introduce _____ (your partner's name) from _____ (your partner's native country)."

INFORMATION WORKSHEET

1. Name_____

2. Native country _____

3. Length of time in the United States _____

4. Occupation _____

5. Family members in the United States _____

   _____

   _____

6. Favorite weekend activities _____

   _____

7. Other classes this semester _____

   _____

8. Something you and your partner have in common

   _____

   _____

9. Something very interesting about your partner

   _____

   _____

To start your sentence, use a phrase from the left column. To finish your sentence, use a phrase from the right column. Or finish the sentence with a phrase of your own. Write the phrases in the spaces provided.

THINGS THAT MAKE YOU ANXIOUS

I felt (feel) anxious about	not knowing the answer to a question
I was (am) frightened of	being the last one picked for a team
I was (am) afraid of	being short (or tall)
I was (am) scared of	being the center of attention
I feared (fear)	being called to the school's office
Some may fear	getting a low grade

_____

_____

_____

_____

_____

_____

THINGS THAT YOU MAY LOOK FORWARD TO

I was (am) looking forward to	meeting new friends
I was (am) excited about	learning new things
I was (am) happy about	getting new books

_____

_____

_____

_____

_____

_____

Preparing a Monologue Tape

▶ **MRS. WOODS: PLEASE, TAKE NOTES!**

Abdul, Eiko, Maria, and Thien listen to Mrs. Woods, their ESL instructor, discuss the first speaking project. Which students might remember the most from the lecture? Which students might remember the least?

Help with Vocabulary

Read each sentence. Write the number of the sentence that the **bold** word is in next to the definition. Then, after each definition, write the word and indicate its *part of speech* (verb (v.), noun (n.), adjective (adj.), preposition (prep.), adverb (adv.), or idiom). Follow the example.

1. Working so many hours can **hinder** his ability to get good grades.
2. What is a good **strategy** for test taking?
3. One **advantage** of living outside the city is fresh air.
4. One **disadvantage** of living in the city is polluted air.
5. Children need to be taught not to **interrupt** adults who are talking.
6. Listen to my speech, and give me some **feedback.** How can I improve the speech?
7. The football players may not like it, but the coach is right to **challenge** them.
8. If you don't study, you may **end up** with a bad grade.
9. He was confused about the directions and asked for **clarification.**
10. She is an **enthusiastic** teacher who can excite her students.
11. I didn't get a good look at him. I only **glanced** at him for a moment.

____ a. an explanation used to make something clear   _____

____ b. a benefit, good point   _____

____ c. input, information   _____

_1_ d. to make difficult, to block or obstruct   ____hinder (v.)____

____ e. to dare to confront, to urge or provoke   _____

____ f. to break off, to cause someone to stop   _____

____ g. to look at something quickly   _____

____ h. a plan or tactic   _____

____ i. to result in   _____

____ j. able to create interest or excitement   _____

____ k. inconvenience, hindrance, bad point   _____

Correct your answers by discussing them or by checking the Answer Key.

PART I: FOCUS ON LISTENING
Mrs. Woods: Please, Take Notes!

From *It's Still a Mom's Life* by David Sipress. Copyright © 1993 by David Sipress. Used by permission of Dutton Signet, a division of Penguin Books USA, Inc.

- What is this cartoon saying about communication?
- Is there a difference between hearing and listening?
- To really listen and understand, what must a person do?

▶ PRE-LISTENING TASK 1

A. Write down four things that you can do to improve your understanding of a lecture.

Sitting in the front row, so I can see, hear, and stay alert

_____

_____

_____

B. Write down four things that might **hinder** your understanding of a lecture.

Thinking about other things and daydreaming about the weekend

_____

_____

_____

C. Discuss your lists from Steps A and B with the entire class.

A. If you don't understand something in a lecture, what is the best **strategy** you can take? Put a check mark (✓) next to the best suggestions in the following list.

_____ 1. If I hear a new word, I can look up the word in my dictionary during the lecture.

_____ 2. I can quietly ask a classmate to explain what I don't understand.

_____ 3. I can look confused and hope the instructor notices me.

_____ 4. I can raise my hand and ask the instructor to explain the point.

_____ 5. I can write down what I thought the instructor said and ask about it when the lecture is finished.

_____ 6. I can tape-record the lecture and listen to it again if I need to.

_____ 7. I can keep quiet and hope to understand the point later.

_____ 8. I can ask a friend to explain the lecture after class.

B. Find a partner, and discuss the **advantages** and **disadvantages** of each suggestion in Step A.

C. Correct your answers by discussing them or by checking the Answer Key.

D. Number 4 is one of the better strategies. Why might an instructor want a student to **interrupt** with a question? Write *T* for True and *F* for False next to each of the following statements.

When a student interrupts a lecture with a question,

_____ 1. the question shows the instructor that the students are listening and thinking.

_____ 2. the question may help other students who have similar questions.

_____ 3. the question disturbs the instructor and the class, and it wastes time.

_____ 4. the question gives the instructor **feedback** about what the students do not understand.

_____ 5. the question will make the instructor angry because it is a **challenge** and the student may **end up** with a bad grade.

E. Correct your answers by discussing them or by checking the Answer Key.

F. In the following space, write a question that you might ask an instructor in class. Ask for **clarification** of something. (Refer to the "Useful Expressions" box at the end of this chapter for help in forming the sentences needed for this activity.)

_____

_____

G. Discuss your questions with the entire class.

▶ LISTENING TASK 1

A. Listen to the instructions. In the spaces provided write down the main ideas.

Name of project _____   Due date _____

Topic _____

Requirements _____

_____

_____

Suggestions for preparation _____

_____

_____

_____

Grading criteria _____

_____

_____

_____

B. Listen to the instructions again, and add more details to the main ideas.

C. Correct your answers by discussing them or by checking the Answer Key.

▶ POST-LISTENING TASK

A. With one other classmate, discuss any questions you have about the instructions on the tape.

B. Write down the questions you would ask about the instructions.

_____

_____

C. Ask your instructor any questions you have about the instructions.

▶ LISTENING TASK 2

A. Listen to Eiko's tape. In the following box, check (✔) each point that she covers.

B. Discuss your answers in Step A with the entire class.

C. Repeat Steps A and B for the tapes of Thien, Maria, and Abdul.

	Eiko	Thien	Maria	Abdul
1. Introduction	___	___	___	___
2. Family and country	___	___	___	___
3. Reasons for coming	___	___	___	___
4. Current situation	___	___	___	___
5. Hopes and dreams	___	___	___	___
6. Conclusion: This class	___	___	___	___

D. In the following box, evaluate the tapes as though you were the instructor. For each student, put a check mark (✔) next to the points that were done well, and leave blanks if the points were not done well. Your instructor may want you to listen to the tapes another time. In the last blank, write a letter grade for each student.

	Eiko	Thien	Maria	Abdul
Was the student's tape:				
on topic?	___	___	___	___
well organized?	___	___	___	___
interesting?	___	___	___	___
loud and clear?	___	___	___	___
well practiced?	___	___	___	___
enthusiastic?	___	___	___	___
spoken freely and not read?	___	___	___	___
OK in pronunciation?	___	___	___	___
OK in grammar?	___	___	___	___
5 to 10 minutes long?	___	___	___	___
GRADE	___	___	___	___

E. Correct your answers by discussing them or by checking the Answer Key.

PART II: FOCUS ON SPEAKING
Preparing a Monologue Tape

Overview: In the monologue tape project, you will record a self-introduction of 5 to 10 minutes. Begin with an introduction: state your name and native country, and give a general idea of the topics you will discuss. Then expand your self-introduction by discussing your native country and your life there. Next discuss why you came to the United States. Talk about your current situation and your hopes for the future. Finally, in your conclusion, state the reason you are taking this class.

A. On the outline on page 23, write out a few important words or phrases under each point. You will turn in the outline with your tape on the due date.

B. Practice recording yourself a few times, guided by your outline. Do not write out your entire monologue, and do not read it. Talk freely and **glance** at your outline only occasionally. Listen to your tape and improve its content and presentation based on the instructor's grading criteria. (Consider playing some music from your native country softly in the background of your recording.)

C. Make your final tape. Be sure that your self-introduction lasts at least 5 minutes. Present it enthusiastically, in a voice that is loud and clear.

D. Label your tape with your name, class, and the date. Rewind the tape and turn it in with the outline on the due date, which is _____.

▶ SPEAKING TASK 2

A. Move your desks so that they form a circle within another circle, like a doughnut. The desks forming the outer circle should face the desks that form the inner circle. Both circles must have the same number of desks.

B. Sit down facing another student.

C. Study the topics of conversation listed on page 20. Begin a conversation with your partner by greeting him or her. Then continue your conversation by discussing the topics listed.

D. Locate your native country on the map on page 21 and show it to your partner. Write down your partner's name and native country in the blanks under "People I met today."

E. Ask as many of the questions suggested under "Topics of conversation" as possible. You may also ask questions that are not listed.

F. Close the conversation with your partner quickly but politely when you hear that the time is up (after 3 minutes).

G. Students sitting in the *outer* circle of desks should stand up and move one seat to the *right* to find a new partner. Those sitting in the inner circle do not move. Now start another 3-minute conversation, repeating Steps C through F.

People I met today

	Name		*Country*
1.	_____	from	_____
2.	_____	from	_____
3.	_____	from	_____
4.	_____	from	_____
5.	_____	from	_____
6.	_____	from	_____
7.	_____	from	_____
8.	_____	from	_____
9.	_____	from	_____
10.	_____	from	_____

Topics of conversation

1. *Greeting* (For example: Hi, how are you?)

2. *Name* (You might need to ask: How do you spell that?)

3. *Native country* (Make sure your partner knows where the country is on the map.)

4. *Length of time in the United States* (For example: How long have you been here?)

5. *Family situation* (For example: Do you live with your family? Are you married? Do you have children?)

6. *Occupation or Major* (For example: Are you working? What's your major?)

7. *Any interesting question* (For example: If you could go anywhere in the world right now and do anything you wanted, where would you go and what would you do? Or: What is your favorite movie?)

8. *Closing* (For example: It was nice talking with you. Let's talk again later.)

Map of the World

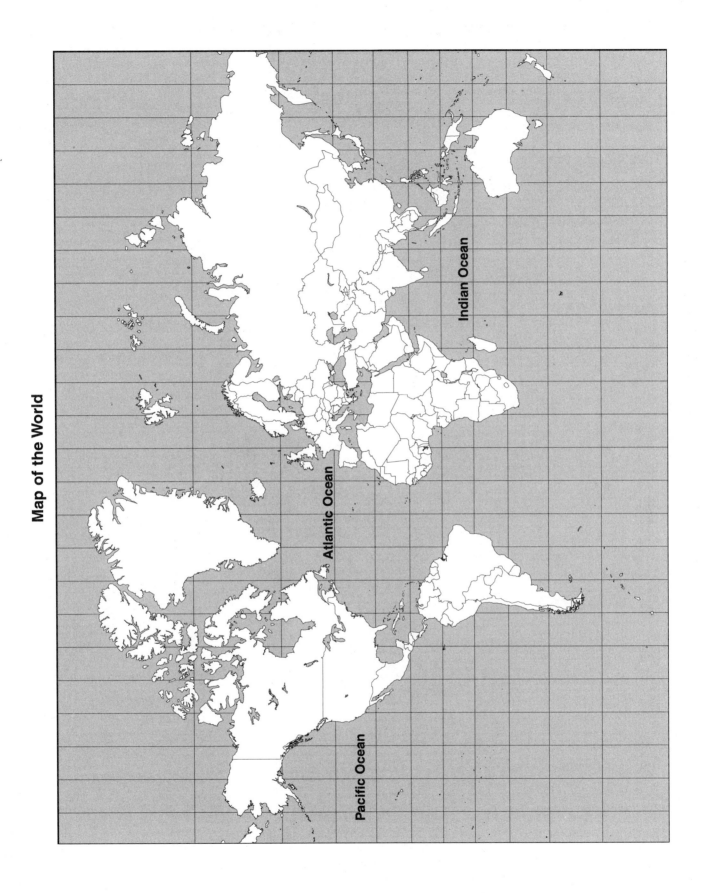

Indian Ocean

Atlantic Ocean

Pacific Ocean

Useful Expressions

ASKING FOR CLARIFICATION

I am not sure I understood. Did you say…?

ASKING FOR REPETITION

Can you please repeat that part about…?

ASKING ABOUT A WORD

I don't know the meaning of _____. Can you spell it and define it for me?

ASKING FOR INFORMATION

Can you tell me when (what, where, how, why)…?

THE MONOLOGUE TAPE

Name _____   Date _____

1. Introduction _____

   _____

2. Family and country _____

   _____

3. Reasons for coming to the United States _____

   _____

4. Current situation _____

   _____

5. Hopes and dreams for the future _____

   _____

6. Conclusion: How this class will help _____

   _____

INSTRUCTOR'S COMMENTS ABOUT CONTENT, PRESENTATION, AND MECHANICS

General comment _____

   _____

Was the student's tape:

on topic? _____

well organized? _____

interesting? _____

loud and clear? _____

well practiced? _____

enthusiastic? _____

spoken freely and not read? _____

OK in pronunciation? _____

OK in grammar? _____

5 to 10 minutes long? _____

rewound? _____   labeled? _____   on time? _____

Conducting a Survey

▶ **ABDUL: FULL-TIME STUDENT, FULL-TIME CASHIER**

Abdul is taking a break from his job at the mini-market. He is returning a telephone call to his uncle. Uncle Muneeb, who **sponsors** Abdul in the United States, is worried about the young man's **hectic** schedule. What questions do you think Uncle Muneeb might want to ask Abdul about his work and school?

Help with Vocabulary

Match the words and their definitions.

_9_	1. **survey**		a.	usual, common
____	2. **sponsor**		b.	to support a person financially
____	3. **hectic**		c.	busy, frantic, disordered
____	4. **typical**		d.	at different times, every so often
____	5. **hold down a job**		e.	to a little degree, slightly, not very much
____	6. **as a matter of fact**		f.	to be enough to pay for
____	7. **workload**		g.	a questionnaire used to learn people's opinions
____	8. **pretty**		h.	somewhat, very
____	9. **kind of**		i.	to be able to keep a job
____	10. **cover the cost**		j.	introduces an example or information
____	11. **from time to time**		k.	the amount of work one has to do

Write the correct vocabulary word from above and indicate its part of speech (verb (v.), noun (n.), adjective (adj.), adverb (adv.), or idiom) in each of the following sentences. Follow the example.

12. I _____ like him, but I'm not sure if he likes me, so don't say anything.

13. The instructor said that she would call the student _____ .

14. I like his music. _____ , I have most of his CDs.

15. A _____ workday for me begins at 8 A.M. and ends at 5 P.M.

16. To _____ while being a full-time student is challenging.

17. They did a _____ survey (n.) _____ to see how many people drive after drinking.

18. He has a heavy _____ . I doubt if he'll have time to help us.

19. You did _____ well. You should be proud of yourself.

20. I've had a _____ day. I was so busy that I didn't have a minute to sit down.

21. My paycheck does not even _____ of my tuition this semester.

22. He agreed to _____ me in the United States. He will pay for my rent and tuition.

Correct your answers by discussing them or by checking the Answer Key.

PART I: FOCUS ON LISTENING

Abdul: Full-Time Student, Full-Time Cashier

- Why can't this young student meet with her teacher now?
- What does this cartoon suggest about the American way of life if even children have to check their calendars?

▶ **PRE-LISTENING TASK**

A. Find a partner, and discuss the following questions:

1. What is a **typical** day like for you here in the United States? (What do you do each day?)
2. Is your life more hectic here in the United States than it was in your country?

B. Jot down the advantages and the disadvantages of having a full schedule.

Advantages of a full schedule   *Disadvantages of a full schedule*

_____   _____

_____   _____

_____   _____

C. Discuss your answers with the entire class.

📼 **A.** Listen to the conversation between Abdul and Uncle Muneeb. Then jot down the main ideas.

Uncle Muneeb's concerns

_____

_____

_____

Abdul's reactions

_____

_____

_____

B. Discuss your answers with the entire class.

▶ **POST-LISTENING TASK**

📼 **A.** Listen again to the conversation between Abdul and his uncle. Then circle the best answers.

1. Why did Abdul call his uncle?

   a. He wanted to learn how his uncle was doing.
   b. He was returning a call from his uncle.
   c. He wanted to thank his uncle for paying his tuition.

2. Uncle Muneeb thought Abdul was calling from

   a. somewhere other than work.
   b. school.
   c. work.

3. Uncle Muneeb was surprised Abdul was calling at that time because

   a. he knew that was the time Abdul was supposed to be at work.
   b. Abdul had taken so long in returning his call.
   c. Abdul never calls him.

4. Uncle Muneeb had called Abdul to learn whether

   a. he needed anything and was doing OK with his hectic schedule.
   b. he was at work.
   c. he had called home recently.

5. Abdul feels that his most difficult class is his

   a. ESL class.
   b. computer class.
   c. business class.

6. Uncle Muneeb suggests that Abdul should

    a. ask to copy another student's notes.

    b. try to see his professor during office hours.

    c. quit his job.

7. Uncle Muneeb thinks that Abdul's business professor is

    a. a boring lecturer.

    b. a woman.

    c. a man.

8. Abdul would like

    a. to pay for his own books from the money he earns at the mini-market.

    b. to be paid more often, rather than from time to time.

    c. to let Uncle Muneeb pay for his books.

B. Correct your answers by discussing them or by checking the Answer Key.

PART II: FOCUS ON SPEAKING
Conducting a Survey

▶ **PRE-SPEAKING TASK 1**

Overview: The speaking project for this chapter is a **survey.** Look at the survey form shown at the end of this chapter to get an idea of what you will be doing. This project has three steps:

1. Form groups of five. As a group, choose a topic and narrow it down. Then choose two types of people to survey, and write five specific multiple-choice questions about the topic.

2. As an individual, find ten people who are willing to be surveyed. Approach those people, and ask them the survey questions. Record their answers on the survey form.

3. As a group, analyze the survey results collected by all group members. Then, as an individual, choose one question and prepare pie graphs and bar charts to report the survey results to the class.

A. Study the following general topics. Choose two general topics that you will narrow down. As shown in the examples that follow, write your general topics in the blanks provided, and then narrow them down.

		General Topics for Survey		
humor	hobbies	games	pets	music
family life	death	male or female roles	friendships	bad habits
professions	dating	superstitions	health	marriage
the elderly	customs	TV viewing	politics	travel
work	shopping	weekend activities	holidays	use of time
eating	studying	religion	sports	exercise

EXAMPLES

General topic: <u>studying</u>

          <u>studying</u> narrowed to <u>study habits</u>

          <u>study habits</u> narrowed to <u>study habits of college students</u>

General topic: <u>family life</u>

          <u>family life</u> narrowed to <u>child raising</u>

          <u>child raising</u> narrowed to <u>methods used to discipline children</u>

General topic: <u>health</u>

          <u>health</u> narrowed to <u>AIDS</u>

          <u>AIDS</u> narrowed to <u>beliefs about preventing the spread of AIDS</u>

General topic: _____

          _____ narrowed to _____

          _____ narrowed to _____

General topic: _____

          _____ narrowed to _____

          _____ narrowed to _____

B. Form groups of five, and discuss the topics that each member has narrowed down. As a group, select one topic that every member will do the survey on. You will survey two types of people — for example, native English speakers and non-native English speakers (or boys and girls; or young people and old people; or married people and single people; or smokers and non-smokers; and so on). It is important that the types of people suit your topic. Each group member will survey five people of each type to see whether and how their habits and attitudes differ. If necessary, define the two types of people you will survey. For example, what do the group members mean by "young" and "old"? "Young" could be defined as those age 20 and under, and "old" could be defined as those age 40 and over. In the following blanks, write your group's topic and the two types of people each student will survey.

Topic _____

Types to survey _____

_____

Abdul's group has chosen "studying" as a general topic. The group narrowed down this general topic to "college students' study habits." Abdul's group will survey working students and non-working students. The group has defined a "working student" as someone who works more than 20 hours a week and takes at least 12 units of classes. So before Abdul begins his survey, he has to ask some questions to determine whether a particular student fits the survey. When he has done that, he can ask questions that both working students and non-working students can answer. The question in the first example asks about a habit.

EXAMPLE 1

Question
How many hours do you study each week?

Possible Answers
A. 0-5 hours   B. 6-10 hours   C. 11 hours or more

It is also good to include questions that ask about attitudes, as shown in the following example.

EXAMPLE 2

Question
Which statement best summarizes your feelings about working and studying?

Possible Answers
A. Students should not work at all.
B. Working part-time is OK.
C. Working and studying are good because they give you practical experience and income.

C. Write two multiple-choice questions and three possible answers about your topic.

1. _____

   _____

   A. _____ B. _____ C._____

2. _____

   _____

   A. _____ B. _____ C._____

D. Discuss the questions as a group, and suggest ways to improve them. Be sure that each question is clear and easy to understand.

E. As a group, choose six or seven of the questions, and write them on a piece of paper. Give your questions to the instructor, who will select the five best questions.

F. When the instructor has approved the questions, each group member should write them on the survey form. Put one question on each page. It is very important for each group member to copy the questions in the same order and to use the exact same words for each question. See the second page of Abdul's survey form on page 35 as an example.

G. Practice saying the questions aloud. Ask the instructor for help if you have trouble with any of the words.

► **PRE-SPEAKING TASK 2**

Now that task 1 is finished (selecting a topic, defining two types of people to survey, and writing the questions), you are ready for task 2: finding people to survey and approaching them politely. Begin by thinking about where you may find the types of people who may be willing to answer your questions.

A. Put a check (✔) mark next to the people and situations that would encourage practicing English and an ✗ next to those that would not. At the bottom of the list, add a type of person or situation that you have found to be a good or a bad choice, based on your own experience.

_____ a foreign student who is taking a break in class

_____ a secretary in a busy office

_____ a coworker who is working

_____ a neighbor who is walking a dog or pushing a baby in a stroller

_____ an elderly person in a retirement home

_____ a group of students who are talking and laughing in the cafeteria

_____ a stranger sitting next to you on a bus

_____ a person sitting alone in a park or waiting for a bus

_____ a person you have met at a health club, market, club, or public place

_____ a person waiting at the Department of Motor Vehicles

_____ _____

B. Discuss your answers in Step A with the class.

C. Approaching the people to interview may seem difficult, but it will be easier if you know what to say. When you have found a person who seems willing to be surveyed, you must politely ask whether he or she has the time and the interest to speak with you. It is important to: (1) identify yourself, (2) state why you want to speak with the person, and (3) mention how much time the conversation might take. In the following blanks, write what you would say to a stranger who might be willing to talk with you. Be sure to include all three points mentioned.

1. _____

_____

2. _____

_____

3. _____

_____

D. Write the sentences from Step C on the board and discuss them as a class. Work with the class and the instructor to correct the grammar of the sentences. Then copy the sentences that you might feel comfortable saying. Ask your instructor to say the sentences aloud, and repeat them to improve your pronunciation. (Refer to the "Useful Expressions" box at the end of this chapter if needed.)

E. Find a partner and role-play the following situations using the sentences you copied in Step D. Your partner may either agree to do the survey or may refuse to do it. If your partner agrees, ask one of the survey questions. If your partner refuses to do the survey, what would you say to him or her? Then switch roles and role-play again. If you feel that you need help with pronunciation, ask your instructor. Here are the role-playing situations:

  a. A young person in a laundry room who looks bored
  b. An elderly person sitting on a bench at a bus stop
  c. A classmate during break

F. Volunteer to role-play in front of the class.

G. Think about someone you know who could do the survey. Write his or her name in the following space. Also name a place you know where you could meet with people who are willing to be surveyed.

_____

_____

▶ **SPEAKING TASK**

A. To practice and get a start on your homework, find a few classmates to survey. After asking them for their time, ask any questions you need to know in order to decide whether they fit the types of people needed for the survey.

B. Ask the survey questions and take notes. Do not ask those being surveyed to fill in the blanks. Be sure that they understand each question and that you understand each answer. Be careful to record their answers in the correct section on your form. All the answers from the first type of people (working students) will be recorded on the top half of the survey form; answers from the second type (non-working students) will be recorded on the bottom. Add up the number of responses for each answer (A, B, and C) and write that down in the space marked subtotal. This is the line you will copy onto the summary form later in this chapter. The survey forms for you to use are on pages 41–51.

C. Continue this process outside of class for homework until you have found ten people to survey.

D. Bring the survey form to class on the date it is due, and discuss it with your group.

The due date for having all five questions answered by ten people is _____.

Note: You will do the survey for homework. However, Post-Speaking Tasks 1 and 2 will be done in class.

On the opposite page is an example of how to fill in the survey form. This is the second page of Abdul's survey. Note that he recorded the results of only one question on this form.

My name <u>Abdul</u>

Question 1 <u>How many hours do you study each week?</u>

_____

_____

Put a check mark (✔) to the right of each person's name to show what answers he or she chose. Mark only one answer for each question.

Type I — All these people are <u>working students.</u>

Name	Possible Answers		
	A. 0-5 hours	B. 6-10 hours	C. 11 or more hours
1. Sue	✓		
2. Mike		✓	
3. Paula		✓	
4. José	✓		
5. James			✓
Subtotal	2	2	1

Type II — All these people are <u>non-working students.</u>

Name	Possible Answers		
	A. 0-5 hours	B. 6-10 hours	C. 11 or more hours
1. Lisa		✓	
2. Magda			✓
3. Mei			✓
4. Vu		✓	
5. Tony		✓	
Subtotal	0	3	2

A. Join your group, and discuss the experience of conducting the survey. What did you like about it? What did you learn? How did you feel about talking to strangers?

B. Discuss the results of the survey in your group. Were the answers what you expected? Were the answers of the two types of people you surveyed different or similar?

C. Each group member should choose one question to analyze. Then collect the pages from other group members so that you have all fifty answers for the one question you will analyze. Add up the subtotals and copy them onto the form called "Summary of Answers." The form for you to use is on page 53. The following is Abdul's survey summary for the first question. Use it as an example.

Abdul chose to collect the results for survey question 1. He copied the subtotals from his own survey and from the surveys of the other four group members and added them up. He will compare the results in the form of a bar graph and pie charts. Because there were 25 people surveyed in each group, he multiplied the subtotal by 4 to get the percentage.

SUMMARY OF ANSWERS
Question ___1___

Question   How many hours do you study each week?

In the blanks under each answer, copy the subtotals from each group member's survey.

Type I Working students

Group Member	Answer A	Answer B	Answer C
1. Abdul	2	2	1
2. Eiko	1	3	1
3. George	2	3	0
4. Maria	3	1	1
5. Jan	2	2	1
Total	10 (40 %)	11 (44 %)	4 (16%)

Type II Non-working students

Group Member	Answer A	Answer B	Answer C
1. Abdul	0	3	2
2. Eiko	1	2	2
3. George	1	1	3
4. Maria	0	2	3
5. Jan	1	1	3
Total	3 (12 %)	9 (36 %)	13 (52 %)

▶ POST-SPEAKING TASK 2

After you have added the subtotals, you are ready to make the bar graph and the pie charts. See Abdul's work that follows on page 38.

A. Bar graph: First, write the the answers to A, B, and C and the totals for Type I and Type II on the horizontal axis as Abdul has done. For the bar graph, use the *number* of responses. Then, draw the bars to the correct height for each answer. Color the bars to show contrast.

B. Pie charts: Write the types of people surveyed for Type I and Type II above each pie. For the pie charts use the *percentages* and not the numbers. Put *A* just to the left of the center, and put *B* just to the right of the center. *C* will fall somewhere between the two. (Note the marks on the edge of each pie; each mark represents 10 percent. Use these marks to determine where to draw the dividing lines in each pie.)

C. Write a conclusion underneath the graph and the charts to summarize your survey. Then, prepare a large version of the graph and charts to use when you report your survey results to the class.

Your report is due on _____.

▶ POST-SPEAKING TASK 3

A. Listen to Abdul's report about survey question 1. This is a model for you when you report on your question. Look at the bar graph and pie charts as he speaks about them.

B. As a class, discuss what Abdul did to make the information he presented understandable to his audience.

C. Form groups and practice giving your report to your group. Each report should take only a few minutes.

D. When you are asked to give your report to the entire class, tape the enlarged version of your bar graph and pie charts on the chalk board. Point out the main findings and state your conclusion.

BAR GRAPH

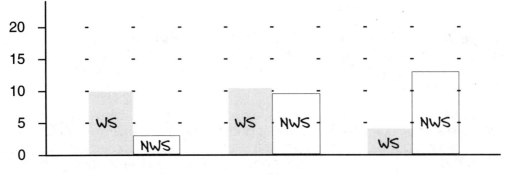

Number of People

20 ·
15 ·
10 ·
5 ·
0

WS   NWS   WS   NWS   WS   NWS

A. ___0-5 hours___   B. _6-10 hours_   C. _11 or more hours_

TI _10_ WS TII _3_ NWS   TI _11_ WS TII _9_ NWS   TI _4_ WS TII _13_ NWS

PIE CHARTS

Type I _Working students_   **Type II** _Non-Working students_

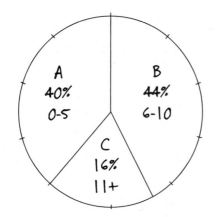

A
40%
0-5

B
44%
6-10

C
16%
11+

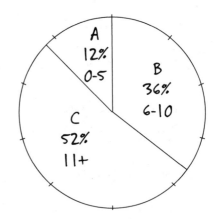

A
12%
0-5

B
36%
6-10

C
52%
11+

Conclusion: Non-Working students study more hours per week than working students.

OPENING AND STATEMENT OF PURPOSE TO SOMEONE YOU KNOW

Hi _____. How are you doing? I wonder if you could do me a favor. I have to do a survey for my English class. Would you mind if I ask you a few questions?

OPENING AND STATEMENT OF PURPOSE TO A STRANGER

Hello. My name is _____. I'm a student at _____. I have to do a survey for my English class. Do you have a few minutes to answer five questions about the topic of _____?

SURVEY COVER PAGE

My name _____   Date _____ Grade _____

Topic of survey _____   Types to survey _____

Question to ask to get the person's permission to survey

_____

_____

_____

Question to ask to determine whether the person fits the type needed for the survey

_____

_____

_____

Type I — All these people are _____

Name	Country	Sex	Age
1. _____	from _____	_____	_____
2. _____	from _____	_____	_____
3. _____	from _____	_____	_____
4. _____	from _____	_____	_____
5. _____	from _____	_____	_____

Type II — All these people are _____

Name	Country	Sex	Age
1. _____	from _____	_____	_____
2. _____	from _____	_____	_____
3. _____	from _____	_____	_____
4. _____	from _____	_____	_____
5. _____	from _____	_____	_____

My name _____

Question 1 _____
_____
_____

Put a check mark (✔) to the right of each person's name to show what answers he or she chose. Mark only one answer for each question.

Type I — All these people are _____

Name   Possible Answers

        A. _____   B. _____   C. _____
        _____   _____   _____

1. _____   _____   _____   _____
2. _____   _____   _____   _____
3. _____   _____   _____   _____
4. _____   _____   _____   _____
5. _____   _____   _____   _____

          Subtotal _____   _____   _____

Type II — All these people are _____

Name   Possible Answers

        A. _____   B. _____   C. _____
        _____   _____   _____

1. _____   _____   _____   _____
2. _____   _____   _____   _____
3. _____   _____   _____   _____
4. _____   _____   _____   _____
5. _____   _____   _____   _____

          Subtotal _____   _____   _____

My name _____

Question 2 _____

_____

_____

Put a check mark (✔) to the right of each person's name to show what answers he or she chose. Mark only one answer for each question.

Type I — All these people are _____

Name   Possible Answers

A. _____   B. _____   C. _____

_____   _____   _____

1. _____   _____   _____   _____

2. _____   _____   _____   _____

3. _____   _____   _____   _____

4. _____   _____   _____   _____

5. _____   _____   _____   _____

Subtotal _____   _____   _____

Type II — All these people are _____

Name   Possible Answers

A. _____   B. _____   C. _____

_____   _____   _____

1. _____   _____   _____   _____

2. _____   _____   _____   _____

3. _____   _____   _____   _____

4. _____   _____   _____   _____

5. _____   _____   _____   _____

Subtotal _____   _____   _____

My name _____

Question 3 _____

_____

_____

Put a check mark (✔) to the right of each person's name to show what answers he or she chose. Mark only one answer for each question.

Type I — All these people are _____

Name	Possible Answers		
	A. _____	B. _____	C. _____
	_____	_____	_____
1. _____	_____	_____	_____
2. _____	_____	_____	_____
3. _____	_____	_____	_____
4. _____	_____	_____	_____
5. _____	_____	_____	_____
Subtotal _____	_____	_____	_____

Type II — All these people are _____

Name	Possible Answers		
	A. _____	B. _____	C. _____
	_____	_____	_____
1. _____	_____	_____	_____
2. _____	_____	_____	_____
3. _____	_____	_____	_____
4. _____	_____	_____	_____
5. _____	_____	_____	_____
Subtotal _____	_____	_____	_____

My name _____

Question 4 _____

_____

_____

Put a check mark (✔) to the right of each person's name to show what answers he or she chose. Mark only one answer for each question.

Type I — All these people are _____

Name   Possible Answers

A. _____   B. _____   C. _____

_____   _____   _____

1. _____   _____   _____   _____

2. _____   _____   _____   _____

3. _____   _____   _____   _____

4. _____   _____   _____   _____

5. _____   _____   _____   _____

Subtotal _____   _____   _____

Type II — All these people are _____

Name   Possible Answers

A. _____   B. _____   C. _____

_____   _____   _____

1. _____   _____   _____   _____

2. _____   _____   _____   _____

3. _____   _____   _____   _____

4. _____   _____   _____   _____

5. _____   _____   _____   _____

Subtotal _____   _____   _____

My name _____

Question 5 _____

_____

_____

Put a check mark (✔) to the right of each person's name to show what answers he or she chose. Mark only one answer for each question.

Type I — All these people are _____

Name   Possible Answers

         A. _____   B. _____   C. _____

         _____   _____   _____

1. _____   _____   _____   _____

2. _____   _____   _____   _____

3. _____   _____   _____   _____

4. _____   _____   _____   _____

5. _____   _____   _____   _____

        Subtotal _____   _____   _____

Type II — All these people are _____

Name   Possible Answers

         A. _____   B. _____   C. _____

         _____   _____   _____

1. _____   _____   _____   _____

2. _____   _____   _____   _____

3. _____   _____   _____   _____

4. _____   _____   _____   _____

5. _____   _____   _____   _____

        Subtotal _____   _____   _____

SUMMARY OF ANSWERS

Question _____

Question _____

_____

In the blanks under each answer, copy the subtotals from each group member's survey.

Type I _____

Group Member	Answer A	Answer B	Answer C
1. _____	_____	_____	_____
2. _____	_____	_____	_____
3. _____	_____	_____	_____
4. _____	_____	_____	_____
5. _____	_____	_____	_____
Total	_____ (%)	_____ (%)	_____ (%)

Type II _____

Group Member	Answer A	Answer B	Answer C
1. _____	_____	_____	_____
2. _____	_____	_____	_____
3. _____	_____	_____	_____
4. _____	_____	_____	_____
5. _____	_____	_____	_____
Total	_____ (%)	_____ (%)	_____ (%)

BAR GRAPH

Number of People

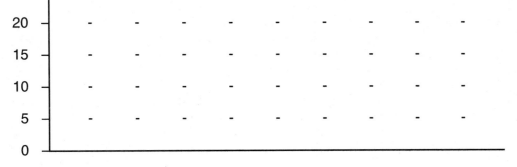

20 –
15 –
10 –
5 –
0

A. _____

TI _____ TII _____

B. _____

TI _____ TII _____

C. _____

TI _____ TII _____

PIE CHARTS

Type I _____

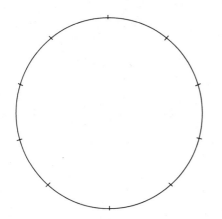

Type II _____

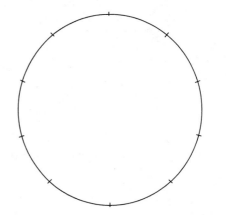

Conclusion:

Writing a Movie Review

▶ **MARIA: TOO MUCH, TOO LATE**

Maria speaks with a friend about being **discouraged.** What might be some of Maria's **concerns** as an older student and mother who is returning to school?

Help with Vocabulary

Read each sentence. Write the number of the sentence that the **bold** word is in next to the definition. Then, after each definition, write the word and indicate its *part of speech* (verb (v.), noun (n.), adjective (adj.), preposition (prep.), adverb (adv.), or idiom). Follow the example.

1. I am **discouraged** about my grades. I don't think I will pass the class.
2. I have a **concern** about the party, and I need to discuss it with you.
3. She will **encourage** me to try again. She said many people fail the first time.
4. I have developed a **tolerance** for his smoking. It doesn't bother me as much now.
5. Everyone I know is married with children. As a single guy, I don't **fit in.**
6. That movie was a real **tearjerker.** I used up a whole box of tissue.
7. **Just the fact that** he called you tells you that he is thinking of you.
8. You must **take** this **seriously.** One more *D* and you will fail the class.
9. She is so **dedicated** to her new job that she even worked on Christmas.
10. You should **take advantage of** his office hours and get help.
11. I know this is a hard class for you, but **hang in there.** It will get easier.
12. The house is not too expensive. As a matter of fact, the price is very **reasonable.**

_____ a. to not give up; to persevere, continue, carry on _____

_____ b. problem, worry _____

_1_ c. sad, troubled, depressed _____discouraged (adj.)____

_____ d. to cheer up, comfort, assure _____

_____ e. used to introduce evidence or proof _____

_____ f. to use to one's own benefit _____

_____ g. to sense or have a feeling of belonging _____

_____ h. to act in a way that shows something is important _____

_____ i. fair, right, sensible, rational _____

_____ j. devoted to _____

_____ k. the ability to endure, to accept but not share _____

_____ l. a movie that makes you want to cry _____

Correct your answers by discussing them or by checking the Answer Key.

PART I: FOCUS ON LISTENING

Maria: Too Much, Too Late

10-17

"They're done! HA HA! *All* the school lunches are done for the next 186 days! No more getting up at 6 a.m.! No more messy sandwiches! No more...."

• Why has this mother made 186 school lunches in one day?

• What is the father doing? Why?

• What does the mother need?

▶ **PRE-LISTENING TASK**

A. When your friends are discouraged, what do you do to **encourage** them? When you are discouraged, what do you want your friends to do for you? Sometimes people simply want you to listen to their problems — that alone will help them feel better. Refer to the "Useful Expressions" box at the end of this chapter, and then role-play with a partner two of the situations in the following list. In one role-play, play the person with the problem. Then play the listener and sympathizer in the other role-play. Before you offer any suggestions, practice listening to the problem carefully, restating the problem, and sympathizing. You may find this hard to do. Decide when it might be best not to suggest a solution at all. Here are the role-playing situations:

1. You got an *F* on a test, and you feel depressed.
2. You forgot about an assignment that is due today, and you feel terrible.
3. You got fired from your job, and you are not sure why.
4. You want to quit your job because of an unfair supervisor.
6. You lost your girlfriend (or boyfriend) because you have to study so much.
7. You feel homesick, and you want to return to your native country.
8. You got a ticket for speeding, and you think it isn't fair.
9. Your husband never helps around the house, and you need more help.
10. Your in-laws demand too much of your free time, and you are frustrated.

B. Volunteer to perform your role-play in front of the class.

C. As a class, discuss whether the listener listened, restated the problem, and sympathized before he or she offered suggestions.

▶ LISTENING TASK 1

With your books closed, listen to the following conversation between Maria and her classmate Mei. Then, as a class, discuss the following two questions.

1. What is Maria concerned about?
2. What does Mei say to encourage Maria?

▶ LISTENING TASK 2

A. Good language learners develop a **tolerance** for not being able to understand every word, and they focus on the main idea. In this exercise, some of the key words are missing. Listen to the tape again and fill in the missing words, some of which you studied in the "Help with Vocabulary" box.

MEI: Hi, Maria. How are you doing? You look _____. Is

1
everything OK?

MARIA: Oh, hi, Mei. I'm fine. Well, _____, just OK, I guess.

2

MEI: Just OK? What is it that's _____ you? Your classes?

3

MARIA: Well, yeah, kind of. I mean … to tell you the _____, I

4

feel, I'm feeling a little _____.

5

MEI: I'm sorry to hear that. What's got you down?

MARIA: I have a few _____ about attending school.

6

MEI: Are you saying you are _____ about your grades?

7

MARIA: Not so much that. My grades are _____ good. It's just

8

that I feel that I don't really _____. I'm more than twice

9

your age, Mei, and I have _____ and all, and everyone

10

else, well….

MEI: Maria! Your age doesn't _____. I think it's great you're
in school. _____ you are here has
_____ all of us. And not only that, you work hard and
are so _____.
                    14

MARIA: Really? The other students think I work hard? They don't think I should be at
home? Maybe I _____. I shouldn't
                              15
worry so much.

MEI: Your feelings are _____. I would probably feel the same
                              16
way, but _____. Why don't you do something to get
           17
your mind off it? Hey, Maria. Let's _____ our day off
                                          18
this week and watch a movie.

MARIA: A movie? What kind? I'm not in the mood for a _____.
                                                            19
A sad drama would make me feel worse.

MEI: And I hate science _____ and horror films, so that leaves
                              20
an action-adventure film or maybe a _____ comedy?
                                          21
Popcorn, soda, no kids, no homework. Come on Maria!

MARIA: OK, OK, Mei. I'm _____ better already. Give me a call
                              22
on Friday, and we'll _____ a movie. And thanks
                          23
for listening.

MEI: You'd do the _____ for me. Talk to you on Friday.
                        24
Bye, Maria.

MARIA: Bye, Mei.

B. Correct your answers by discussing them or by checking the Answer Key.

▶ POST-LISTENING TASK

A. Maria talked about her concerns with a friend before they became real problems.
Discuss the following questions as a class:

1. If Maria had come to you, what would you have told her?
2. Who else could give Maria some help or encouragement?
3. Would you go to a school counselor for help? Why or why not?
4. Who do you go to when you need encouragement and help?

PART II: FOCUS ON SPEAKING
Writing a Movie Review

"I want an action-adventure film, she wants a romantic comedy.
I just don't see how we can resolve this!"

- What problem is this couple at the video store having?
- Do video stores really have video counselors?
- Who chooses what videos to watch at your house?

▶ PRE-SPEAKING TASK 1

Watching movies on video can be a fun way to learn English. However, there are more than ten thousand movies available on videos, so finding one that you will enjoy can be a challenge. The first way to narrow down your choices is to consider which kinds of movies you enjoy. Movies are classified in different categories.

A. Form groups of four, and discuss the following categories of films. In the spaces provided, write the name of one movie that your group thinks fits into each category. If you are unsure what some of the categories mean, ask your instructor.

Film categories	*Title of movie*
Action-Adventure Films	_____
Children's / Family Films	_____

Comedies   _____

Documentaries   _____

Dramas   _____

Foreign-Language Films   _____

Horror Films   _____

Musicals   _____

Mystery / Suspense Films   _____

Science-Fiction / Fantasy Films   _____

Westerns   _____

B. Discuss your group's answers with the entire class.

Another consideration in selecting a film is its **rating.** Since November 1967, movies have been rated G, PG, PG-13, R, and X by the Motion Picture Association of America. These ratings give viewers, and parents of young viewers, some idea of how violent or adult the content of a movie is.

C. As a class, discuss what the following abbreviations mean and write their meanings in the blanks. Check your answer by discussing them or by checking the Answer Key.

G _____   R _____

PG _____   PG-13 _____

X _____

Another kind of rating shows how film critics evaluated a movie. Many critics use the following "star" rating system:

     ✶✶✶✶✶ = **Excellent**

      ✶✶✶✶ = **Very Good**

       ✶✶✶ = **Good**

        ✶✶ = **Fair**

         ✶ = **Poor**

D. The films listed on the next page are considered very good or excellent by movie critics and also show some aspect of U.S. culture that may interest ESL students. Check (✔) the films that you have already seen. Discuss those movies with your group. (Refer to the bottom of the "Useful Expressions" box at the end of this chapter for help in forming questions and comments related to movies.)

Film	Category	Rating	Year	Main Actor	Notes
____ Beaches	Drama	PG-13	'88	Bette Midler	tearjerker, musical, friendship
____ Big	Comedy	PG	'88	Tom Hanks	13-year-old in 35-year-old body, fantasy
____ Chariots of Fire	Drama	PG	'81	Ben Cross	English Olympic runners in 1924
____ Children of a Lesser God	Drama	R	'86	William Hurt	deaf woman
____ My Cousin Vinny	Comedy	R	'91	Joe Pesci	lawyer, small town in Alabama
____ Dances with Wolves	Western	PG-13	'90	Kevin Costner	Civil War, Sioux
____ El Norte	Drama	R	'93	Zaide Gutierrez	Spanish language, illegal immigrants
____ Fiddler on the Roof	Musical	G	'71	Topol	old values, changing world
____ Forrest Gump	Drama	PG-13	'94	Tom Hanks	six Academy Awards
____ The Fugitive	Action-Adventure	PG-13	'93	Harrison Ford	murder
____ The Gods Must Be Crazy	Comedy	–	'80	Marius Meyers	Africa
____ Gone with the Wind	Drama	PG	'39	Clark Gable	most-loved film in the United States
____ It's a Wonderful Life	Drama	–	'46	James Stewart	classic, Christmas
____ The Joy Luck Club	Drama	R	'93	Kieu Chin	cross-cultures, generation gap
____ Kramer vs. Kramer	Drama	PG	'79	Dustin Hoffman	divorce and custody
____ The Last Emperor	Drama	R	'87	John Lone	3-year-old Qing emperor
____ La Bamba	Musical	PG-13	'87	Lou Diamond Phillips	Ritchie Valens's story
____ Little Women	Drama	PG	'95	Winona Rider	sisters growing up together
____ Mr. Mom	Comedy	PG	'83	Michael Keaton	mom and dad role reversal

Film	Category	Rating	Year	Main Actor	Notes
____ *My Fair Lady*	Musical	–	'64	Rex Harrison	British class system, language
____ *My Left Foot*	Drama	R	'89	Daniel Day-Lewis	handicapped Irish writer
____ *One Flew over the Cuckoo's Nest*	Drama	R	'75	Jack Nicholson	mentally ill
____ *Places in the Heart*	Drama	PG	'84	Sally Field	widowed mother
____ *The Princess Bride*	Family	PG	'87	Carry Elwes	romance, fairy tale
____ *Rainman*	Drama	R	'88	Dustin Hoffman	autistism, brothers
____ *Ran*	Foreign Language	R	'85		Japanese with subtitles, sixteenth century warlords
____ *Robin Hood Prince of Thieves*	Action-Adventure	PG-13	'91	Kevin Costner	
____ *Schindler's List*	Drama	R	'93	Liam Neeson	World War II, Nazi death camps
____ *The Shawshank Redemption*	R	Drama	'95	Tim Robbins	innocent prisoner
____ *Steel Magnolias*	Drama	PG	'89	Sally Field	tearjerker, friendship
____ *West Side Story*	Musical	–	'61	Natalie Wood	Romeo-Juliet theme
____ *Witness*	Mystery/ Suspense	R	'85	Harrison Ford	culture clash
____ *Working Girl*	Comedy	R	'88	Melanie Griffith	working one's way up

E. Select a group member to report to the class about the movies your group discussed.

▶ **PRE-SPEAKING TASK 2**

A. On the next page is Maria's review of the movie *Stand and Deliver*. Read it and discuss it as a class.

MOVIE REVIEW

Name Maria Sanchez   Date September 12, 1997

Name of the movie Stand and Deliver   Year of the movie 1988

Rating of the movie (G, PG, PG-13, R) PG   Awards of the movie _____

Your rating _____★★★★★_____ (Use a five-star scale: 1 star = bad, 3 = OK, 5 = great.)

▼ Setting (where and when the story takes place) The setting is 1982 at East Los Angeles
High, an inner-city school filled with violence and kids that society and most of the teachers
have given up on. Since the film is based on a true story, the setting is very realistic.

▼ Major characters and a brief description (Put actors' names in parentheses.)
The main character is Jamie Escalante (Edward James Olmos), a dedicated math teacher
who believes that kids will rise to the level of what one expects of them. He believes in his
students and has the gift of teaching. He inspires eighteen students to move from basic math
to passing a calculus exam. Angel (Lou Diamond Phillips) is one of the students who is changed
by Escalante. He passes the AP calculus exam with high marks despite the fact that he
is a gang member struggling with economic and social problems.

▼ Plot (what happens) The story begins as Escalante quits a higher-paying job to teach at
Garfield High, a school where the students are in control and have little respect for authority.
He soon captures the hearts of his students by his strange teaching methods, and he decides
to teach them calculus. He works with them weekends and holidays and even suffers a
heart attack. His students pass the exam, which is a first for Garfield High. The students
are accused of cheating and have to retake the exam to prove their innocence.

▼ Issues (what the movie is saying about life) Two issues that the film deals with are
discrimination and determination. The students are mostly Hispanic, and one reason they
are accused of cheating is because of their last names. Escalante teaches them that
despite the unfairness of the system, they can succeed. This touches on the other issue
the film deals with, determination. With hard work and a strong sense of belief in themselves,
the students learn that they can accomplish their dreams. Escalante never stops believing
in them, and they in turn learn to believe in themselves.

▼ Opinion (What the best part was, and what the worst part was)
The best part of the film was when the principal received the marks of the students after
the re-test. It was so exciting to see the students vindicated. I didn't enjoy the violence in
the film or the disrespect shown to the teachers.

▼ New vocabulary AP = Advanced Placement, self-esteem = confidence in one's abilities,
cajole = coax, talk into, persuade

MOVIE REVIEW

Name _____   Date _____

Name of the movie _____   Year of the movie _____

Rating of the movie (G, PG, PG-13, R) _____   Awards of the movie _____

Your rating _____ (Use a five-star scale: 1 star = bad, 3 = OK, 5 = great.)

▼ Setting (where and when the story takes place) _____
_____
_____

▼ Major characters and a brief description (Put actors' names in parentheses.)
_____
_____
_____
_____
_____
_____

▼ Plot (what happens) _____
_____
_____
_____
_____
_____

▼ Issues (what the movie is saying about life) _____
_____
_____
_____
_____
_____

▼ Opinion (What the best part was, and what the worst part was)
_____
_____
_____

▼ New vocabulary _____
_____

▶ PRE-SPEAKING TASK 3

A. Choose a movie from the list that you haven't seen but would like to see.

B. Rent the movie from a video store, and watch it outside of class.

C. Complete every section on the Movie Review form. (The form is on page 67.) Look up a few new words you heard in the film, and jot down the definitions.

The due date for your movie review is _____.

▶ SPEAKING TASK

A. After you have turned in your movie review, listen to Maria reporting to her small group about the movie *Stand and Deliver*.

B. Form groups of four, and give an informal report, like Maria's, about the movie you saw. Discuss the following points: setting, major characters, plot, issues, your rating, and your favorite part. Feel free to ask your classmates questions about the movie.

C. Select one group member to report to the class about the movies the group discussed.

One way to encourage someone is to listen to his or her problem carefully, restate what you hear the problem to be, sympathize with the person, and possibly suggest a solution.

RESTATING THE PROBLEM

You sound as though you are really _____ about _____.

Are you saying that you _____?

SYMPATHIZING WITH THE PERSON

I'm sorry to hear that. You must feel terrible.

That's too bad. It isn't easy when that happens.

No wonder you are feeling that way. I would be _____ too.

SUGGESTING A SOLUTION

You might try talking to _____.

Have you tried _____?

What are you going to do about it? Maybe you can _____.

EXPRESSIONS USED IN DISCUSSING MOVIES

Have you seen any good movies lately?

Have you seen the movie _____?

What kind of movies do you like?

What rating does the movie have?

Did you read any reviews? I heard that the movie got "two thumbs up."

It was a box-office hit.

I heard it was a box-office flop.

The special effects are great, but the acting and the plot are weak.

Don't tell me how it ends; I haven't seen it yet.

I think I'll wait to see it when it comes out on video.

CHAPTER 5

Conducting an Interview

▶ **EIKO: THIS STRANGE COUNTRY!**

Eiko is writing in her journal about some of her problems adjusting to life in the United States. What might some of her concerns be?

Help with Vocabulary

Cover up the definitions at the bottom of this box. As you listen to the instructor read each sentence, guess the *meaning* of the **bold** word and its *part of speech* (verb, noun, adjective, adverb, preposition, or idiom.) After each sentence, discuss which context clues helped you make your guess.

1. Let's **celebrate** after graduation by having a party at my house!
2. Her daughter goes to **UCLA** and majors in Political Science.
3. She is in the **homestay** program offered by the university.
4. I don't feel like cooking. Let's eat some **leftovers.**
5. I will **help myself** to some coffee and wait for the meeting to begin.
6. My child's smile can **cheer** me **up** when I come home from a hard day.
7. Add flour to the soup to give it a thicker **consistency.**
8. In that **analogy,** people are ingredients, and society is soup.
9. The **vertical** blinds you put on the windows look great.
10. The line across the bottom of the graph is the horizontal **axis.**
11. Although I understand his views, I can't **adopt** them as my own.
12. She made a **tragic** mistake and let her child out of the car seat.
13. The **horizontal** stripes on his shirt make him look muscular.
14. The president would not **negotiate** on that point at all.

Write the correct number of the sentence above that the **bold** word is in next to the definition. Then, write the word and indicate its part of speech (verb (v.), noun (n.), adjective (adj.), adverb (adv.), preposition (prep.), or idiom). Follow the example.

____ a. to make someone who is sad feel better   _____

____ b. upright, straight up and down   _____

_1_ c. to have a good time in honor of an achievement   _celebrate (v.)_

____ d. to bargain   _____

____ e. from left to right or side to side   _____

____ f. firmness or thickness of a liquid   _____

____ g. to serve yourself   _____

____ h. terrible, sad, unfortunate   _____

____ i. a line on which things are drawn symmetrically   _____

____ j. prepared food that has not been consumed and is saved   _____

____ k. University of California at Los Angeles   _____

____ l. a program that houses foreign students with native families   _____

____ m. to take in   _____

____ n. a comparison of two things in order to explain a point   _____

Correct your answers by discussing them or by checking the Answer Key.

PART I: FOCUS ON LISTENING
Eiko: This Strange Country!

"I tell ya, meals used to be such a pain in the neck!
Now, thanks to the vending machines, they're a breeze.
No more cooking, no more dirty dishes. ..."

- What has this mother done to save herself from cooking at home?
- What does this cartoon say about how some people in the United States may feel about meal times and cooking?
- What was difficult for you to get used to regarding meals and eating in the United States?

▶ PRE-LISTENING TASK

Predict three specific problems that Eiko or any foreign student might have living with an English-speaking family in the United States. Discuss your predictions with the class.

▶ LISTENING TASK 1

A. Listen to Eiko as she reads from her journal. Write down three of her concerns.

1. _____

2. _____

3. _____

B. Read the following statements. Then listen again to Eiko as she reads from her journal. Write *T* for True and *F* for False next to each statement.

_____ 1. Today is special for Eiko because it is her older brother's birthday.

_____ 2. Eiko couldn't reach her family in Japan by phone.

_____ 3. Eiko has gotten three *A*'s on projects in her ESL class.

_____ 4. Eiko feels that she has a lot in common with Cindy, her homestay "sister."

_____ 5. Eiko has to interview several English speakers born in the United States for her project.

_____ 6. The hardest thing for Eiko about living in the United States is that she misses her family.

_____ 7. Eiko thinks it is fun to live in a home where people eat at different times and places.

_____ 8. Eiko used to enjoy helping her mother prepare the meals in Japan.

_____ 9. Eiko liked it that Jennifer and Cindy at least tried to eat some Japanese food at a restaurant, because now they know how she feels eating strange foods.

_____ 10. Eiko goes for a walk when she doesn't understand the jokes her homestay family tells.

_____ 11. Eiko cries because she misses her family and has a hard time with English.

_____ 12. What makes Eiko really happy is letters from her boyfriend.

C. Correct your answers by discussing them or by checking the Answer Key.

▶ **POST-LISTENING TASK 1**

A. Recall your first day in the United States and how you felt about what you saw. What was the strangest thing you experienced? Does it still seem strange to you today? Why or why not?

B. Tell a partner your experiences in "this strange country."

C. Share some of the stories with the class.

▶ **POST-LISTENING TASK 2**

A. Adjusting to a new culture is called *acculturation,* and it is not easy. Discuss the following questions as a class:

1. What does it mean to "adjust to a culture"? Give some specific examples of adjusting.

2. Is the goal of acculturation for a person to become as much like the culture as possible? If not, then what is the goal?

3. What are the advantages of retaining some of the customs, values, and beliefs of your native culture? Give some specific examples.

4. What are the disadvantages of rejecting all the customs, values, and beliefs of your native culture? Give some specific examples.

5. What are the disadvantages of rejecting all the customs, values, and beliefs of the new culture? Give some specific examples.

6. What are the advantages of **adopting** some of the customs, values, and beliefs of the new culture? Give some specific examples.

B. The traditional idea about acculturation in the United States was represented by a melting pot or soup. In other words, many different ingredients (many ethnic groups) were all put into one pot (the United States), and they gradually took on an even **consistency** and one flavor (a common way of doing things). Now many prefer to use the **analogy** of the salad bowl. In this view of acculturation, each ingredient retains its distinctive flavor (Chinese, Mexican, African-American), and at the same time each enhances the flavor of the salad by giving it variety (ethnic diversity). Discuss the following questions:

1. What are the problems with using these analogies to describe acculturation?

2. Do you have any analogies of your own to describe acculturation?

C. Consider your acculturation process as you study Eiko's graph. At the top of her **vertical axis** is a 10, which means that she is comfortable with the changes she has had to make and has accepted the this country's way as one way of doing things; she understands, to a degree, the reasons behind the changes. It does not mean she will adopt all aspects of U.S. culture and forget her own. That would be **tragic**. At the bottom of Eiko's graph is a 1, representing a low score, which means that she feels she is among strangers and does not want to fit in or know how to. Eiko arrived in the United states in April 1996, and she made the graph in October 1997; she filled in the other dates evenly, every three months.

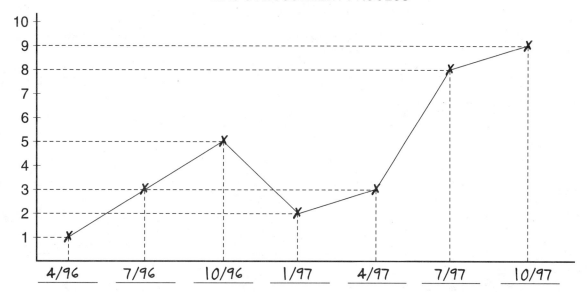

EIKO'S ADJUSTMENT PROCESS

D. Fill out the graph that follows to show your own acculturation process. On the first blank on the **horizontal** axis, write the month and year that you first arrived in the United States. On the last blank, write the current month and year. Fill in any dates that seem important to you, dates that marked either high points or low points in your acculturation.

E. Discuss your graph with another student. Explain the importance of the dates in your graph.

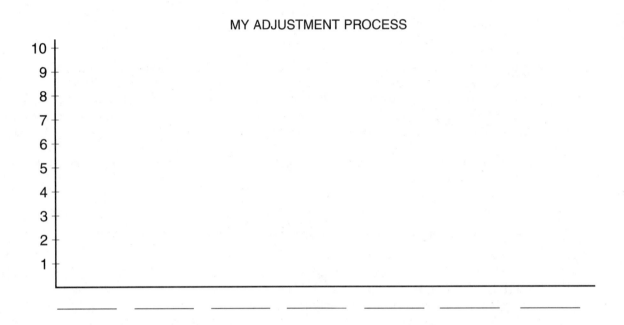

MY ADJUSTMENT PROCESS

▶ **POST-LISTENING TASK 3**

A. Think of suggestions that you would give to a foreign student or a relative from your native country who is coming to the Unites States to study English. Consider the person's academic, social, personal, and professional life. What would you tell him or her about adjusting to life in the United States?

B. Write some of your suggestions in complete sentences, as shown in the example.

1. Don't give up if you can't understand much at first; you'll get it, but it takes time!

2. _____

3. _____

4. _____

5. _____

6. _____

7. _____

8. _____

9. _____

10. _____

C. Discuss your suggestions with a small group. If time permits, also discuss them with the entire class.

▶ **LISTENING TASK 2**

A. Close your book and listen to the non-native English speaker interview a native speaker. As shown by an asterisk (*) in the following tapescript, there are some errors in the non-native speaker's English. Notice how the two speakers **negotiate** the meaning of what they say so that they can understand each other.

B. Keep your book closed and listen again to the interview. Then discuss with the class the strategies the two speakers used to negotiate meaning. What did they do to make sure that they understood each other?

C. Study the following five strategies that these speakers used to negotiate meaning. Did you mention all of them?

1. Interrupt the speaker with a specific question.
2. Ask a question by repeating the statement with rising intonation.
3. Ask for repetition of a specific phrase or word.
4. Give feedback to show you understand.
5. Give feedback to control the pace of the conversation.

In the parentheses ( ) after some of the sentences and questions in the tapescript, write the number of the strategy that the speaker used. The first one is done for you.

NON-NATIVE SPEAKER: Do you ever tell to a friend to borrow you some money?*

NATIVE SPEAKER: Borrow you some money? (2) Do you mean "lend you" some money? ( )
Do I ever ask my friends *to lend* me money? ( )

NON-NATIVE SPEAKER: Yes. *Lend you* money; that's what I mean. ( )

NATIVE SPEAKER: Well, it all depends on, you know, how well I know them, and all. Like, if they owe me any favors and stuff like that. I mean I would, I guess, if I really needed it and it wasn't that much, say $20 or $40. But I wouldn't go around borrowing $200 from friends. Besides, who has that much cash to give away these days? When I need....

NON-NATIVE SPEAKER: Excuse me. I'm confused a bit. Is your answer yes or no? ( ) I have to write down yes or no.

NATIVE SPEAKER: Let's say yes. That is, if it's under 50 bucks, a good friend, and I really need it.

NON-NATIVE SPEAKER: Could you repeat that last part a bit slower, please? ( ) and ( )

NATIVE SPEAKER: I'm sorry. I speak fast, don't I? I borrow money if it is under $50, if I'm borrowing from a good friend, and if I really need the money. Just write yes.

D. Correct your answers by discussing them or by checking the Answer Key.

E. Read the following cartoon and discuss the questions.

- What is the husband playing on the tape recorder, and why?
- What would happen if the tape stopped?
- What strategy is illustrated by this cartoon?

▶ **POST-LISTENING TASK 4**

A. Do you remember the contract that you made in Chapter 1? The contract was about making changes so that you would have more opportunities to speak English. Turn to the contract on page 9 in Chapter 1 and see what you wrote.

B. Share with the class any successes you have had in finding ways to speak English outside the classroom.

C. Who was your partner in the exercise when you discussed the contract in Chapter 1? If you remember, after class ask him or her, "How is the contract from Chapter 1 going?" or "Have you found more opportunities to speak English?"

PART II: FOCUS ON SPEAKING
Conducting an Interview

A. Study the following topics, and circle one that you find interesting.

watching sports	starting a business	losing weight
movie stars	investing money	taking vacations
getting exercise	shopping for bargains	finding a job

B. Write three information questions about the topic you chose. Begin your questions with words like *What, Who, Why, When, Where, How many,* etc. (Don't answer the questions now.)

1. Question _____

_____

   Answer _____

_____

2. Question _____

_____

   Answer _____

_____

3. Question _____

_____

   Answer _____

_____

C. Ask a partner your questions, and write down his or her answers. To be sure you understand each other, remember to use the following strategies for negotiating meaning. (Refer to the "Useful Expressions" box at the end of this chapter if needed.)

1. Interrupt the speaker with a specific question.
2. Ask a question by repeating the statement with rising intonation.
3. Ask for repetition of a specific phrase or word.
4. Give feedback to show you understand.
5. Give feedback to control the pace of the conversation.

D. When you have finished the interview, ask your partner to check the answers you wrote down to see if you understood what he or she said.

▶ PRE-SPEAKING TASK 2

Overview: This project, conducting an interview, is like the survey you did. In both cases, you are asking someone questions and recording their answers. However, this interview is different from the survey in several ways. In the interview, you ask questions of only one person. Also, your questions are not multiple-choice questions; they are information questions that may lead to longer and more involved answers. Therefore, you might consider tape-recording the interview so that you can concentrate on the person you are interviewing; you can write the answers down later as you listen to the tape. Another difference between the interview and the survey is that you do not work in a group. This gives you greater freedom in choosing the topic and the type of person to interview. You should be very selective in choosing a topic and the person to interview. *Think of someone who has accomplished something that you want to accomplish. Ask how he or she did that thing and what he or she would do differently now.* Eiko, for example, interviewed a Japanese student at her college who had learned English quickly and seemed to have adjusted easily to U.S. culture. Eiko wanted to learn her secrets and wondered whether she, too, had difficulties at first. Maria was hoping to interview Patty Hernández, one of the counselors at the college. Maria respected Patty because she had returned to school and completed her degree while holding down a job. Also, Patty was known for her activities in helping minority women accomplish their goals.

A. In choosing someone to interview, consider as many possibilities as you can. Write them in the spaces provided.

Someone in the field that you are majoring in _____

Someone working in the career that you are considering _____

Someone who has faced and met a challenge you are currently facing _____

Someone you admire _____

Someone you want to know more about _____

Someone who knows about a topic you are interested in _____

Other ideas _____

B. Write a few questions about the topic you may use in your interview.

_____

_____

_____

C. Find a partner and discuss your topics and questions. Get feedback on ways to improve the questions, and ask for suggestions for other questions. Predict what the answers will be.

D. As a class, discuss some of your topics, questions, and predictions.

▶ SPEAKING TASK

A. Fill in the interview form by writing out a narrowed-down topic and ten specific questions about it. Questions that can be answered by yes or no are acceptable if you follow them with "Why?" The form is on pages 83–84.

B. Make sure your questions are grammatically correct, and practice saying the questions aloud. Get help with pronunciation if you need it.

C. Review Chapter 3 about how to approach people and ask for their time. In this case, you must identify yourself and state what you are doing, why you have selected that person to interview, and how long you expect the interview to last. The interview might take 20 or 30 minutes, so you may need to make an appointment with the person.

D. Ask your questions and take notes. Do not ask the person being interviewed to fill in the blanks. If you plan to record the interview, ask for permission by saying something like, "Do you mind if I record the interview?" Check that the tape recorder is working before you begin the interview. You may ask more questions that come to mind during the interview, but you don't have to.

E. Turn in the interview form on the due date, which is _____.

▶ POST-SPEAKING TASK

Form small groups and discuss any of the following:

1. Your selection of topic, questions, and person interviewed
2. Your thoughts and feelings before, during, and after the interview
3. Your predictions of the answers and the actual answers
4. What you learned from the interview itself (the actual answers)
5. What you learned from the experience of interviewing someone

Useful Expressions

INTERRUPTING

Excuse me. Did you say…?

I don't mean to interrupt, but….

ASKING FOR REPETITION

What was that?

Excuse me?

Pardon me?

Could you repeat that part about…?

GIVING FEEDBACK

Oh, now I see. Uh-Huh.

Could you say that again, a little more slowly?

INTERVIEW

Interviewer _____   Topic of interview _____

Interviewee _____   Date of interview _____

Question 1 _____

_____

_____

_____

Question 2 _____

_____

_____

_____

Question 3 _____

_____

_____

_____

Question 4 _____

_____

_____

_____

Question 5 _____

_____

_____

_____

Question 6 _____

_____

_____

_____

Question 7 _____

_____

_____

_____

Question 8 _____

_____

_____

_____

Question 9 _____

_____

_____

_____

Question 10 _____

_____

_____

_____

Other questions and answers that came up during the interview

_____

_____

_____

_____

_____

_____

_____

What I learned about the topic _____

_____

_____

How I felt about the interview _____

_____

_____

Vocabulary Review

ENTREPRENEUR

strict

Chicken out

Tragic

Strategy

ANXIOUS

ENTHUSIASTIC

Workload

Pretty

demanding

jot down

survey

TYPICAL

Probation

Axis

adopt

Dedicated

Hectic

SPONSOR

TEARJERKER

anxious	jot down	strict	GPA
chicken out	frustrate	keep track of	embarrassed
demanding	down for a nap	entrepreneur	probation
suicide	shift		

Fill in the blanks with the words from the box.

The other day when I was trying to get my two-year-old son _____

___ (to sleep for a short period of time), and was trying to convince my ten-year-old

daughter to do better in math, I told them the story of Mr. Miller, my seventh-grade

math teacher.

"When I was in seventh grade," I began, "I was very _____

___ (worried) about attending school. One reason I worried was because of my math

teacher, Mr. Miller. He was so _____ (enforced rules severely)

that he would lock students out of the room just for being a few minutes late. And not

only that, he would also put them on _____ (a testing period),

which meant that if they were late again, he would drop them from his class. One

day I was late because Mother, your grandma, had to work the late

_____ (period of time at work), and so we had overslept.

Even though I had asked her to _____ (write quickly) a note

explaining why I was late, I would _____ (be afraid to do it)

and not go to class. I was too scared to face Mr. Miller, and too

_____ (ashamed, humiliated) to even tell Mother I had

never gone to class that day. Luckily, no one found out.

Well, Mr. Miller was not only strict, he was also _____
9

(required a lot). He expected all his students to get high grades, a 3.5 to 4.0

_____ (grade-point average). He would always
10

_____ (remember) each student's grades in his mind,
11

and it would _____ (disappoint) him when even one of
12

us got a *B*. Having Mr. Miller for seventh grade was _____
13

(to do something difficult or dangerous intentionally)."

When I finished my story, my son was sleeping. My daughter asked if Mr. Miller was

still teaching. I told her not to worry; he had long retired. I wondered if Mr. Miller

had any idea that one of his most fearful, but now most grateful, students had become

a successful _____ (a person who organizes and manages
14

a business).

glance	disadvantage	feedback	strategy
challenge	end up	advantage	interrupt
clarification	enthusiastic	hinder	

Fill in the banks with the words from the box.

Dear Helpful Advisor,

I need some advice. My boyfriend wants to get married, but I want to wait until

I have finished my college degree. He says that one _____

1

(good point) of getting married now is that we would share the living expenses and

housework and therefore would have more time for our studies. I'm afraid that I'll

_____ (result in) with the majority of the housework,

2

and possibly the expenses too, and will have to drop out of school before I complete

my degree. He is so _____ (excited) about it that I hate to

3

constantly _____ (stop, break off) him to give him negative

4

_____ (input, information). I'm afraid I'll lose him if I

5

_____ (confront) him on this issue. What should I do?

6

Sue

Dear Sue,

From just a _____ (quick look) at your letter, I can

7

see that you are aware that couples who rush into marriage may face a

_____ (bad point). After the honeymoon is over, there would be

8

several problems to work through. Although I would like _____

9

(explanation) on some points — such as how long you two have known each other,

your common goals, and so on — I think it is safe to say that marrying at this time

would _____ (make difficult) your chances of achieving your

10

personal academic goals. I suggest that you come up with a _____

11

(plan) to discuss the issue openly and honestly with your boyfriend. If he loves you, he

will be willing to wait and work out an arrangement so that you both can accomplish

your goals together.

as a matter of fact	hectic	sponsor	typical
cover the cost	kind of	survey	workload
hold down	pretty	from time to time	

Fill in the blanks with the words from the box.

SAM: Joe? Hey, Joe, it's you! Long time no see. Where have you been lately?

JOE: Sam. Hi. Yeah, it has been a while hasn't it? It's good to see you. I've been

_____ (very) busy lately with the extra
          1

part-time job.

SAM: How do you do it?

JOE: It's _____ (somewhat) crazy, but I have to work in
                    2

order to _____ (pay for) of my kid's education.
                  3

_____ (used to begin a phrase with an example
          4

or information), I just mailed another payment.

SAM: That must be _____ (busy, frantic), running around
                              5

trying to _____ (keep under difficult circumstances)
                  6

two jobs.

JOE: It sure is. The _____ (amount of work) is heavy,
                          7

and besides that we _____ (to support financially)
                              8

my cousin from Europe.

SAM: Well, if it makes you feel any better, I just saw a _____
                                                                      9

(questionnaire) that reported that the _____ (usual)
                                                        10

college graduate makes more than twice the income of a non-college graduate.

JOE: Good! Then maybe my son will be able to pay me back someday. That is, if he

ever does graduate.

SAM: He will, Joe. If he is anything like you, he'll do it. Well, I've got to go, but give

me a call. We should get together _____ (every

so often). Let's not become strangers.

JOE: OK, Sam. Good to see you. Bye.

SAM: Bye.

11

concern	encouraging	just by the fact that	tolerate
dedicated	fit in	reasonable	tearjerker
discouraged	hang in there	take advantage of	take seriously

Fill in the blanks with the words from the box.

Are you _____ (sad) about the amount of money you make?
1

Is your life as sad as a _____ (movie that makes you cry)? Do you
2

wonder how long you can just _____ (perseveres, carry on)?
3

Would you like to advance your career but don't know how? Would you like to go back to

school but are afraid you won't _____ (have a sense of belonging)?
4

If you answered "Yes" to any of these questions, then you should

_____ (use for your benefit) the highly successful program
5

"Careers Are Us." At Careers Are Us we _____ (regard as important)
6

every single _____ (worry) you may have about getting a better
7

career. We are _____ (devoted) to _____
8   9

(to comfort, to assure) each and every student. We are known for our patient instructors

as well as our _____ (fair) rates. _____
10   11

(because) you have read this advertisement shows that you are ready for a change. Don't

_____(endure) another day at a dead-end job. Prepare for a real
12

career at Careers Are Us today!

adopt	axis	celebrate	cheer her up	consistency
homestay	horizontal	leftover	negotiate	help herself
vertical	UCLA	tragic		

Fill in the blanks with the words from the box.

One of my students told me a story about what could have been a _____
1
(sad, unfortunate) mistake she made as a foreign student in the Unites States. She was

studying at _____ (University of California at Los Angeles) and was
2

living with an American family as part of the _____ (housing) program
3

offered at that time. The family she lived with was very nice and often tried to

_____ (make her feel better) when they thought she was homesick.
4

They also tried to teach her to _____ (take on) the "American" way
5

of doing things, telling her to _____ (serve herself) to food in the
6

refrigerator and to _____ (bargain) for the rights to the remote
7

control for the TV. One evening the whole family, including the grandparents, had

a dinner party to _____ (have a good time in honor of an achievement)
8

the success of Timmy, the 12-year-old son. Timmy had won first place for his creative

science project, and he was asked to show his grandparents the large graphs on which

he had recorded the data. As he was proudly reported the results of his project, pointing

to the _____ (upright, straight up and down) _____
9   10

(line) and the _____ (going from left to right) _____
11   12

(line), he stopped to ask if they wanted to see the actual substance he had created.

He went to the refrigerator and opened a container, and as he showed everyone

something with the _____ (firmness or thickness) and color of soup,
13

he said, "Hey, who took half of my project. It's half gone!" At this point my student spoke

up and said, "Timmy, I'm really sorry. I thought it was _____ (saved
14

food) soup, and I ate some. Now I know why it tasted so bad!" After Timmy explained

that nothing in his science project was harmful, they all had a long laugh about

the bad-tasting "soup."

CHAPTER 6

Giving an Impromptu Speech

▶ **THIEN: HOMESICK AND SICK OF ENGLISH**

Thien makes an appointment to meet with Mrs. Woods, his ESL instructor. He wants to discuss his grades. What do you think Mrs. Woods might suggest Thien do to improve his grades?

Help with Vocabulary

Match the words and their definitions.

_i_	1.	**impromptu**	a.	near, close by
____	2.	**enormous**	b.	encouragement, reason for taking an action
____	3.	**stressed out**	c.	to go down
____	4.	**slip**	d.	to hate, intensely dislike
____	5.	**adjacent**	e.	to be noticeably different
____	6.	**cannot stand**	f.	a system to select a winner by random drawing
____	7.	**motivation**	g.	favorite, most cherished
____	8.	**or else**	h.	feeling the effects of pressure or stress
____	9.	**confident**	i.	without much preparation, spontaneous
____	10.	**lottery**	j.	sure, positive, certain
____	11.	**fondest**	k.	very big, large
____	12.	**stand out**	l.	introduces a threat or alternative

Write the correct vocabulary word from above and indicate its part of speech (verb (v.), noun (n.), adjective (adj.), adverb (adv.), or idiom) in each of the following sentences. Follow the example.

13. Whenever I get anxious, I get an _____ appetite and eat anything in sight.

14. A student's grades may _____ during periods of stress.

15. His _____ impromptu (adj.) _____ speech was so good that many people thought it had been prepared.

16. Write your name in the first column and your child's name in the _____ column.

17. Her _____ for coming here was to get a better education.

18. You either say you are sorry, _____ I'll leave you.

19. I usually do not gamble, but I like to play the _____ now and then.

20. My _____ memory is of my grandmother brushing my hair.

21. I _____ it when you tell me how to drive. Keep quiet, or take a bus.

22. His blonde hair made him _____ among his Asian classmates.

23. You seem _____ by your problems at work. Why not take a vacation?

24. She was so _____ in what she was saying that I believed her.

Correct your answers by discussing them or by checking the Answer Key.

PART I: FOCUS ON LISTENING

Thien: Homesick and Sick of English

I'm sure you've been reading about the enormous emotional pressures we teenagers are under today, so I know you'll understand when I say I've just been too stressed out to write my history paper.

SIPRESS

From *It's a Teacher's Life* by David Sipress. Copyright © 1993 by David Sipress. Used by permission of Dutton Signet, a division of Penguin Books USA, Inc. and International Creative Management.

- What are this student's reasons for not getting the homework done?
- What might be some of the "**enormous** emotional pressures" that make him **stressed out?**

▶ PRE-LISTENING TASK

A. Thien is going to see his ESL instructor because he knows his grades will **slip.** Think of what problems might be causing Thien's poor grades, and write three of them in the following spaces. Then think of solutions to Thien's problems, and write them in the **adjacent** column.

Problems causing poor grades	*Solutions to the problems*
He doesn't understand the assignments	He could ask a classmate or the instructor

B. Discuss your answers in a group of three. (Refer to the "Useful Expressions" box at the end of this chapter if needed.)

▶ LISTENING TASK

A. Listen to the conversation between Thien and his instructor, and circle all the answers that apply.

    1. **How would you describe the instructor?**

       angry, concerned, understanding, demanding, strict, encouraging, helpful,

    2. **How would you describe Thien?**

       shy, honest, **confident**, embarrassed, confused, happy, stressed out

B. Correct your answers by discussing them or by checking the Answer Key.

C. Read the following questions. After listening to the conversation again, answer them.

    3. What were Thien's concerns? _____

    _____

    4. What was Thien's explanation for his low grades? _____

    _____

    5. What has been Thien's motivation for taking and passing the class so far?_____

    _____

    6. What was Mrs. Woods' plan to help Thien? _____

    _____

D. Correct your answers by discussing them or by checking the Answer Key.

▶ POST-LISTENING TASK

A. With a partner, role-play a teacher/student conference like the one you just heard on the tape. Choose any problem you like, and see whether your partner can suggest a good solution.

B. Volunteer to perform your role-play in front of the class.

PART II: FOCUS ON SPEAKING
Giving an Impromptu Speech

▶ PRE-SPEAKING TASK 1

Overview: In this project you will speak for 2 minutes about a topic assigned to you by the instructor. You will listen carefully to the assignment and will discuss the topic for 2 minutes with another student. Then you will prepare a short impromptu speech at your desk for 2 minutes. You will present your speech to the class when you are selected to do so by the instructor.

Two or three students will speak about each topic, and then you will repeat the process with a new topic and a different partner. The instructor will grade you on the presentation and the content of your speech.

A. Working in groups of four, discuss the dos and don'ts of presenting a speech.

B. Write your ideas about giving an impromptu speech in the spaces provided. Consider such things as the speaker's voice, posture, hand movements, eye contact, and facial expressions.

Do	*Don't*
Act confident and be sure of yourself	Apologize for your nervousness

C. Discuss your ideas about speeches with the class.

▶ PRE-SPEAKING TASK 2

A. With the class, discuss the following elements of a speech. An effective speech should have

1. an opening question or comment that grabs the audience's attention
2. a clearly stated main idea followed by specific support that is organized logically
3. a conclusion that returns to the main idea and includes a final "thank you"

B. Listen to Thien's impromptu speech. With the class, discuss whether Thien's speech had the elements as described in Step A.

C. Listen to Thien's speech again. In the following spaces, fill in the notes that Thien might have written down to speak from. Do not include every word.

Note's from Thien's Impromptu Speech

Attention-grabbing comment or question _____

_____

Clearly stated main idea _____

_____

Body of speech

1. _____

_____

_____

2. _____

_____

_____

3. _____

_____

_____

Conclusion _____

_____

_____

_____

D. Correct your answers by discussing them or by checking the Answer Key.

E. For homework, practice several speeches. First choose one of the topics on the following pages. Then jot down some notes using the outline above. Finally, speak out loud about the topic for 2 minutes.

A. Move your desks into two rows so that they form a semicircle, or a horseshoe. The desks on the outer row of the horseshoe should face the desks on the inner row of the horseshoe. There must be the same number of desks in both rows.

B. Sit down facing another student.

C. Listen to the topic your instructor assigns. Exchange first names and greet your partner. Then begin a 2-minute conversation about your topic. Both of you should speak for about 1 minute.

D. Close your conversation quickly but politely when you hear that the time is up (after 2 minutes).

E. Prepare to present a speech about your topic. Begin by collecting your thoughts and jotting down some notes. After 2 minutes, the instructor may ask for volunteers or may call on students to present their speeches. When it is your turn, go to the front of the class and speak clearly and with confidence. After two or three students have spoken about the topic, a new topic will be assigned, and you will repeat the process.

F. If you are sitting on the outer row of the horseshoe, move one seat to the right. With your new partner, start another 2-minute conversation about the new topic. Those sitting in the inner row do not move.

EXAMPLES OF SPEECH TOPICS

Finish the following sentences by giving three supporting examples.

1. If I won the **lottery,** I would....

2. If I were the president, I would....

3. If I could be anyone, I would be....

4. If I were an animal, I would be a....

5. If I could go back in time, I would go to....

6. If I could change anything about my life, I would change....

7. If I could be anywhere in the world, doing anything I wanted, I would be....

8. If I could change anything about the world today, I would change....

9. If I could change anything in history, I would change....

10. If I could bring back anyone to life, I would bring back....

(Continued on the next page.)

Describe the following topics with vivid, specific details.

11. The best day of my life was....

12. The most romantic date from beginning to end was when (*or* would be)....

13. The qualities of a good friend are....

14. The most embarrassing thing that ever happened to me was....

15. My **fondest** childhood memory was when....

16. My favorite possession is....

17. My best vacation was when (*or* would be)....

18. My dream house would be....

19. My favorite person in all the world is....

20. My most scary experience was when....

Explain what you would do in the following situations, and say why.

21. If my good friend were an alcoholic but he or she did not admit it, I would....

22. If my 16-year-old were skipping classes, I would....

23. If I were told I had three months to live, I would....

24. If my friends and family did not like the person I loved, I would....

25. If I found hundreds of dollars in a bag, I would....

26. If my house caught fire, the three things I would save are....

27. If I knew that a coworker was stealing from the company, I would....

28. If I found out that I had been adopted as a child, I would....

29. If I were the opposite sex, I would....

30. If I were invisible one day, I would....

▶ **POST-SPEAKING TASK**

As a class, discuss which impromptu speeches were well done. What made those speeches **stand out?**

Useful Expressions

EXPRESSING PROBLEMS AND SOLUTIONS

Maybe Thien isn't doing his homework *because he doesn't* understand the directions.

Perhaps he is in the wrong class. *It could be that* the work is too hard for him.

I think it is a personal problem. *I suppose* he is having family or financial problems.

It might help if he had a friend he could study with and could call if he had questions.

I think he needs to meet with the instructor or even a counselor and discuss his situation.

The best solution is for him to make the class a high priority, and to cut out other activities.

ATTENTION-GRABBING DEVICES FOR IMPROMPTU SPEECHES

Have you ever been…? Well, I have, and I will never forget it.

Did you know that everyday someone…?

Imagine that you were….

What would you do if you were…?

A popular saying goes, "…"

STATING THE MAIN IDEA

If I won the lottery, I would do three things.

If I were the president, I would change three laws.

My dream house would have three main features.

STATING MAIN POINTS OR REASONS

First of all, …

Second, …

Finally, …

ADDING SPECIFIC EXAMPLES TO SUPPORT MAIN POINTS

For example, …

For instance, …

To get specific, …

CONCLUSIONS

In conclusion, …

CHAPTER 7

Preparing and Delivering an Effective Speech

▶ **ABDUL: IT'S NOT FAIR!**

You have probably heard some boring speeches or lectures in school. What made the speeches so ineffective? Can you recall a particularly good speech? What made it effective?

Read each sentence. Write the number of the sentence that the **bold** word is in next to the definition. Then, after each definition, write the word and indicate its *part of speech* (verb (v.), noun (n.), adjective (adj.), preposition (prep.), adverb (adv.), or idiom). Follow the example.

1. The hikers **stand in awe** before the beauty of the mountains.
2. They will debate a **controversial** subject like abortion or gun control.
3. I could not **persuade** my mother to let me go on the trip to California.
4. Some people feel the death penalty is not a **deterrent** for crime.
5. His **proposition** is not clearly stated. Is he for abortion or against it?
6. A **relevant** subject to discuss with teenagers is the danger of drug abuse.
7. He has established **rapport** with his students. They listen to his every word.
8. She will **allot** only 10 minutes for each student's oral report.
9. She has a favorite **anecdote** about her children.
10. He did not even try to **refute** the strong arguments made by the lawyer.
11. The newspaper printed **inaccurate** information. The dates were wrong.
12. He is **biased.** He gave the award to his own students, but we deserved it.

____ a. something offered for consideration, a subject to be discussed   _____

____ b. a short, entertaining story   _____

_1_ c. to be amazed, in wonder with fear and respect   _____stand in awe (v.)_____

____ d. debatable, having opposing sides   _____

____ e. a close relationship, agreement, harmony   _____

____ f. to give, set aside for   _____

____ g. having to do with, relating to   _____

____ h. to convince, to talk into   _____

____ i. to prove to be wrong   _____

____ j. not correct   _____

____ k. prejudiced, in favor or against someone   _____

____ l. a hindrance, something that prevents or stops something else   _____

Correct your answers by discussing them or by checking the Answer Key.

PART I: FOCUS ON LISTENING
Preparing and Delivering an Effective Speech

From *It's a Teacher's Life* by David Sipress. Copyright © 1993 by David Sipress. Used by permission of Dutton Signet, a division of Penguin Books USA, Inc. and International Creative Management.

- Did you ever fall asleep during a teacher's lecture?
- When that happens, is it the speaker's fault or the sleeper's fault?

► PRE-LISTENING TASK

A. Study the outline "Preparing and Delivering an Effective Speech" on pages 114–115.

B. From the outline's title, which two things should you be able to do after listening to the speech.

_____   _____

C. Write the six steps needed to do the two things in Step B.

1. _____

2. _____

3. _____

4. _____

5. _____

6. _____

D. Discuss your answers for Steps B and C. Also discuss how an outline helps a speaker organize and prepare a speech and how it might help in delivering the speech.

▶ **LISTENING TASK 1**

A. Listen to Mrs. Woods' entire speech for the first time, and focus on the main ideas. Follow the outline, and jot down notes on the outline itself.

B. Discuss the speech with a partner for 5 minutes, looking at the notes you wrote on the outline. What did you find interesting? What did you not understand?

▶ **LISTENING TASK 2**

A. Listen to only the *introduction and step 1*. Then discuss the following questions with your partner, using the outline and your notes. When you have finished writing your answers, discuss them with the class or check the Answer Key.

1. What is the first sentence of the speech? _____

_____

_____

2. What do you think the first few sentences of the speech might cause the class to

   do? _____

   _____

3. What is the objective of Mrs. Woods' speech? _____

_____

4. What does the speaker try to do in a persuasive speech? _____

_____

5. What is the difference between a persuasive speech and an informative speech?

_____

B. Listen to only *step 2,* and discuss the following questions with your partner, using the outline and your notes. When you have finished writing your answers, discuss them with the class or check the Answer Key.

6. What does it mean "assess your audience"? _____

_____

7. Why is this step important? _____

_____

8. What is rapport, and how can it be measured? _____

_____

9. How does it affect your speech to know your audience's educational level,

profession, and personal information? _____

_____

C. Listen to only *step 3,* and discuss the following questions with your partner, using your outline and notes. When you have finished writing your answers, discuss them with the class or check the Answer Key.

10. What two choices does Mrs. Woods suggest about selecting a topic?

_____

_____

11. What are six or seven things to consider when you select a topic?

_____

_____

_____

12. Why is it important to narrow down your topic? _____

_____

_____

13. What question do you ask yourself in order to narrow down the topic?

_____

_____

D. Listen to only *step 4,* and discuss the following questions with your partner, using the outline and your notes. When you have finished writing your answers, discuss them with the class or check the Answer Key.

14. Why might periodicals be a better source than books? _____

_____

15. What are some other sources of material? _____

_____

E. Listen to only *step 5,* and discuss the following questions with your partner, using the outline and your notes. When you have finished writing your answers, discuss them with the class or check the Answer Key.

16. What type of numbers are used for the major points in a formal outline?

_____

17. What are five ways to grab the attention of your audience? _____

_____

_____

18. The body of the speech should be logically developed. What does that mean?

_____

_____

19. The body must also be adequately supported. What does that mean?

_____

_____

20. What must you be careful about when presenting a controversial topic?

_____

_____

F. Listen to only *step 6*, and discuss the following questions with your partner, using the outline and your notes. When you have finished writing your answers, discuss them with the class or check the Answer Key.

21. What are the three ways that Mrs. Woods suggests you practice your speech?

    _____

    _____

22. Which do you think is the best way for you to practice and why?

    _____

    _____

23. What three or four forms of visual aids are mentioned? _____

    _____

24. What content could be displayed with a visual aid? _____

    _____

25. What are two examples of a specific purpose for a visual aid? _____

    _____

26. What can you do both before and during the speech to overcome poor

    pronunciation? _____

    _____

    _____

27. Why is it a bad idea to memorize the speech? _____

    _____

    _____

28. What does this mean? "The message is only as reliable as the messenger."

    _____

    _____

29. What two words are used to describe how you should stand while giving a

    speech? _____

30. What should your hands and eyes be doing during the speech? _____

    _____

OUTLINE FOR "PREPARING AND DELIVERING AN EFFECTIVE SPEECH"

INTRODUCTION

I. **Step 1: Determine the purpose of the speech.**

    A. To persuade

    B. To inform

    C. To entertain

II. **Step 2: Assess your audience.**

    A. The importance of knowing the audience

        1. Helps in choosing a relevant topic

        2. Helps build rapport

        3. Helps with persuasion

    B. Factors to consider

        1. Education, general world knowledge

        2. Profession, specialty knowledge

        3. Other personal information

III. **Step 3: Select and narrow the topic.**

    A. Select an appropriate and relevant topic

        1. One you know a lot about

        2. One you wish you knew more about

    B. Narrow the topic by determining your objective

IV. **Step 4: Gather material.**

    A. Library

        1. Books

        2. Periodicals

    B. Other sources

        1. Media

        2. Interviews

        3. Lectures

        4. Personal experiences

V. Step 5: Organize the material into an outline.

    A. Outline format

    B. Attention-grabbing device

        1. Question

        2. Thought-provoking statement

        3. Quote

        4. Anecdote

        5. Startling statistic

    C. Body

        1. Logically developed

        2. Adequately supported

    D. Conclusion

VI. Step 6: Deliver the speech based on the outline.

    A. Rehearse

        1. Out loud

        2. On tape

        3. To a critical audience

    B. Visual Aid

        1. Form

        2. Content

    C. Language

        1. Pronunciation tips

        2. Natural or conversation-like

    D. Appearance

Conclusion:

Overview: Writing an effective outline can be a lot of work, but it is worth the effort. An outline helps you see whether you have organized your thoughts, have determined the main ideas, and have supplied sufficient support and examples under each point. Because you will not be permitted to read your speech, an outline will help you deliver the speech; it becomes your guide to speak from. Also, if you provide the outline as a visual aid or handout to your audience, they can follow your speech and review it afterward.

A. The first step in writing an outline is to separate the main points from the supporting points and the examples you will use. For practice, rearrange the following words into outline form. Use the Roman numerals *I* and *II* for the main classification — the two main points. Then use capital letters *A, B, C,* and *D* for the supporting points. Finally, use the numbers *1, 2,* and *3* for the specific examples.

Sisters	Husbands	Aunts	Brother Bill	Females
Uncle Sam	Aunt Cindy	Mothers	Aunt Louise	Uncles
Males	Uncle Dick	Sister Laura	Brother John	Fathers
Sister Karen	Wives	Uncle Bruce	Brothers	Aunt Ann

I. _____   II. _____

_____   _____

_____   _____

_____   _____

_____   _____

_____   _____

_____   _____

_____   _____

B. Correct your answers by discussing them or by checking the Answer Key.

C. Rearrange the following four groups of words into sample outlines for speeches about (1) a disease, (2) a controversial topic, (3) how to do an activity, and (4) a problem in society. Use Roman numerals for the main points and capital letters for the supporting points.

1. Arrange these words into an outline for a speech about a disease (such as alcoholism, bulimia, cancer, AIDS).

   Causes   Brief background   Symptoms   Conclusion
   Introduction   Prevention   Treatment   Definition

   _____

   _____

   _____

   _____

   _____

   _____

   _____

2. Arrange these words into an outline for a speech about a controversial topic (such as gun control, abortion, the death penalty).

   Arguments in favor   Definition   Conclusion
   Introduction   Arguments against   Brief background

   _____

   _____

   _____

   _____

   _____

   _____

3. Arrange these words into an outline for a speech about how to do something (such as lose weight, exercise, quit smoking).

Why it is beneficial   How to do it   Definition
Brief background   Conclusion   Introduction

_____

_____

_____

_____

_____

4. Arrange these words into an outline for a speech about some problem in society (such as gangs, drug abuse, rape, child abuse).

Causes   Prevention   Introduction   Brief background
Definition   Conclusion   Effects

_____

_____

_____

_____

_____

_____

_____

D. Correct your answers by discussing them or by checking the Answer Key.

PART II: FOCUS ON SPEAKING
Abdul: It's Not Fair!

▶ **PRE-SPEAKING TASK**

A. To prepare for your speech, follow the steps with Abdul (steps 1 to 6 in the outline for "Preparing and Delivering an Effective Speech").

B. Determine which type of speech you will prepare: persuasive, informative, or entertaining. Mrs. Woods asked Abdul to choose between an informative and a persuasive speech. Abdul did not want to speak about a controversial topic, so he planned to prepare an informative speech.

Write down which type of speech you plan to prepare: _____

C. Assess your audience. Abdul knew from his survey project that most of his classmates worked. Most of them had middle to low income levels. He also knew that only a few had higher degrees of education; the majority of students were in freshman-level courses. The average age of his classmates was 23, but one woman and one man were much older. The students represented ten countries and many religions. Consider these same factors when you think about your specific audience.

D. Select and narrow the topic. Abdul knew he had to chose a topic that would interest him and his audience. Because most of his classmates worked and because he was having some troubles at work, he decided to speak about workers' rights. He narrowed his topic by deciding what he wanted his speech to accomplish. He wanted his classmates to understand and be able to act on their rights as employees in case they were ever discriminated against at work.

To select your topic, answer the following questions. Write down anything that comes to mind. Explore as many possibilities as you can.

1. What topics do you know a lot about?

   _____

2. What topics do you want to know more about?

   _____

3. What classes do you enjoy?

   _____

4. What shows or exhibits do you like to go to?

   _____

5. What magazines do you like to read?

_____

6. What hobbies do you have?

_____

7. What talents do you have? What awards have you received?

_____

8. What do you like to do in your spare time, on weekends, and on vacations?

_____

9. What current news stories interest you?

_____

10. Look over your answers for questions 1 through 9. Which topics would you and your classmates most enjoy?

_____

11. What would you like your classmates to do, to know, or to believe after your speech?

_____

E. Gather materials. Abdul's class went on a tour to the library. He decided that periodicals (articles from newspapers and magazines) would be most helpful to him, so he used the *Reader's Guide to Periodicals.* He found and photocopied several articles about workers' rights. He also decided to interview a law professor and a counselor on campus.

1. What types of library materials will help you to research your topic?

_____

2. What other kinds of material might you explore?

_____

F. Organize your material into an outline. Abdul read the articles about workers' rights. He highlighted important ideas and wrote notes in the margins. He also wrote notes when he interviewed the law professor and the counselor. He decided to organize his speech into two parts: knowing your rights as a worker and the steps to take when you want to act on your rights. To grab attention, Abdul decided to begin with his own true story of discrimination at work, followed by a clear statement of his purpose. Here is his outline:

I.   Introduction: My true story of discrimination at work

II.   Objective of speech: To be able to identify and act on your rights
as an employee

III.   Knowing your rights

IV.   Acting on your rights

V.   Conclusion

G. Look over the sample outlines you made in the Post-Listening Task, and develop one outline into a model for a speech. Or prepare a new outline, and give it to your instructor for comments.

▶ SPEAKING TASK

A. Practice your speech. Abdul did a great job because he followed the instructor's suggestions in Step 6: He rehearsed out loud in front of a mirror, he recorded his speech, and he gave it to a critical audience. He used a poster-sized outline as a visual aid, and he delivered his speech in a clear and convincing manner. (Refer to the "Useful Expressions" box at the end of this chapter for ideas about moving from one point to another.)

1. What visual aid would best support your speech in terms of both form and content?

   _____

2. Who will listen to you practice your speech? _____

▶ POST-SPEAKING TASK 1

Write notes about each classmate's speech, noting his or her name, topic, and main idea. What did the classmate do well, and what could be improved? (What were the strong and weak points?) If your instructor does not give you copies of the form, copy it by hand, on one side of a sheet of paper. Remember that your comments may be given to your classmates, so be kind and constructive. The form for you to use is on page 127.

After you have read your classmates' comments and have viewed the videotape of your speech (if that was possible), answer the following questions.

Name _____   Date _____

1. What is your general impression of your speech? Why?

   _____

   _____

2. Was your topic appropriate, considering your audience? Why or why not?

   _____

   _____

3. Did the audience like your topic? How do you know?

   _____

   _____

4. Was your attention-grabbing device effective? Why or why not?

   _____

   _____

5. Were the content and organization of your speech clear to the audience?

   _____

6. Did you use your time wisely, or did you have too much or too little to say

   at the end? _____

   _____

7. Were you well prepared? Why or why not? _____

   _____

8. How effective were your eye contact, posture, and use of hands and voice?

   _____

   _____

9. Did your pronunciation or grammar prevent the audience from understanding you? How? _____

_____

10. Did you establish rapport with the audience? How do you know?

_____

_____

11. Did your visual aid help the audience to understand your main or difficult points? How do you know? _____

_____

12. Did you have a confident, definite conclusion to your speech? Write it here.

_____

_____

13. If the audience asked questions, did you understand and answer them?

_____

_____

14. Do you now feel more confident about speaking to a group of people?

_____

15. What will you do differently the next time you give a speech (consider your topic, preparation, and presentation)? _____

_____

_____

BEGINNING A SPEECH

After your attention-grabbing device (such as a question, quote, anecdote, joke, or thought-provoking statement), you may wish to say one the following:

Good Afternoon. My name is _____, and it is my pleasure to be here to speak to you about....

Hello. I'm _____, and today I will speak about....

My name is _____, and after my speech today you will be able to....

REFERRING TO A VISUAL AID

As you can see from the chart here, there are....

If you look at page 2 of the handout, at the top, you will see that....

This chart illustrates my point dramatically. The first bar represents....

MOVING TO ANOTHER POINT

Now that I have discussed the _____ and the _____, I will move on to my final point, the _____.

The next point I wish to make is....

Moving on to point 3, ...

CONCLUDING THE SPEECH

In conclusion, there are....

Thank you.

To summarize, the steps necessary to _____ are first _____, then _____, and finally _____.

So, in conclusion, ...

NOTES FOR POST-SPEAKING TASK

Name of speaker _____

Topic _____

Main idea _____

Strong points _____

Weak points _____

Name of speaker _____

Topic _____

Main idea _____

Strong points _____

Weak points _____

Name of speaker _____

Topic _____

Main idea _____

Strong points _____

Weak points _____

Name of speaker _____

Topic _____

Main idea _____

Strong points _____

Weak points _____

Name of speaker _____

Topic _____

Main idea _____

Strong points _____

Weak points _____

CHAPTER 8

Participating in a Debate

▶ **MARIA: TEAMWORK**

Have you ever seen a formal debate? Have you ever been in one? Soon you will.

Help with Vocabulary

Cover up the definitions at the bottom of this box. As you listen to the instructor read each sentence, guess the *meaning* of the **bold** word and its *part of speech* (verb, noun, adjective, adverb, preposition, or idiom.) After each sentence, discuss which context clues helped you make your guess.

1. Let's **construct** a program to help foreign students find jobs.
2. The 1973 Supreme Court ruling on Roe **versus** Wade made abortion legal in the United States.
3. An unborn child is called a **fetus** from the end of the third month until birth.
4. They **sacrifice** their free time on the weekends to help the homeless.
5. When the prosecution was able to **cross-examine** her, the woman admitted she had killed them.
6. The **offensive** side of the basketball team is responsible for scoring points.
7. The **defensive** side should prevent the other team from scoring any points.
8. She didn't **contribute** money for the ticket, so she doesn't get a share of the prize.
9. I wish we could **abolish** all forms of child abuse.
10. She was in pain and dying, so the family sadly agreed on **euthanasia.**
11. We feel **censorship** of TV is needed in order to reduce violence.
12. The **inmate** told the prison guard that he was sorry for what he had done.
13. It is **mandatory** to wear seat belts in cars. It's not an option any longer.

Write the correct number of the sentence above that the **bold** word is in next to the definition. Then, write the word and indicate its part of speech (verb (v.), noun (n.), adjective (adj.), adverb (adv.), preposition (prep.), or idiom). Follow the example.

_____ a. to give up something of value in order to achieve something else _____

_____ b. in contest against _____

_____ c. to destroy, do away with, end completely _____

_____ d. the act or method of causing death painlessly _____

_____ e. a person who is being held in jail or an institution _____

_____ f. the side of a team that must score points or attack _____

_____ g. to give jointly with a group of others _____

_____ h. a means of examining things to remove objectionable content _____

_____ i. the side of a team that defends the goal or position _____

_____ j. to question closely to find out the truth _____

_____ k. required, something that must be done _____

__1__ l. to plan, make, build _____construct (v.)_____

_____ m. in humans, the unborn young from the end of the third month to birth _____

Correct your answers by discussing them or by checking the Answer Key.

PART I: FOCUS ON LISTENING
Maria: Teamwork

- What does the son plan to tell his father?
- What is he saying first? Why?

This chapter focuses on *debate*, which is a formal argument. Learning to present your points in a clear, convincing manner is a useful skill that can help you win arguments.

▶ PRE-LISTENING TASK

A. One of the most controversial topics in the United States is abortion. Why do you think that it is? What issues are raised by abortion? Discuss this topic with the class.

B. What arguments can you make on both sides of the abortion issue? Find a partner and write three points for each side.

Abortion should be made illegal because:

1. _____

2. _____

3. _____

Abortion should remain legal because:

1. _____

2. _____

3. _____

C. Discuss your points in Step B with the class.

▶ LISTENING TASK

A. Maria and three teammates debated four other classmates about the topic of abortion. Maria's team was arguing against abortion. They wanted to change the current laws that permit abortion. Their proposition was "Abortion should be made illegal in the United States." Listen to the debate and write down a few words that summarize the main points.

Maria's main point: _____

_____

_____

_____

Rosa's main point: _____

_____

_____

_____

Issues raised by classmates' questions: _____

_____

_____

_____

B. Discuss your notes in Step A with the class.

C. Listen to the debate again and add to your notes. Write a question that you would have asked.

_____

_____

_____

D. Correct your answers by discussing them or by checking the Answer Key.

▶ POST-LISTENING TASK

You heard only the first half of the debate, in which the affirmative side constructed its case, the negative side did a cross-examination, and the audience questioned the affirmative side. In the next part of the debate, the negative side would construct its case, be cross-examined by the affirmative side, and then be questioned by the audience. The negative side would argue against changing the current law that permits abortion. What do you think their main points should be? Discuss your ideas as a class.

PART II: FOCUS ON SPEAKING
Participating in a Debate

▶ **PRE-SPEAKING TASK**

Overview: For this speaking project you will be part of a debate team. You will debate a proposition that suggests a change in policy, such as, "The federal government should declare a national holiday in honor of all ESL students." Your team will decide to be either the affirmative side, which supports the proposed change, or the negative side, which is against the change. The team must research the topic; plan offensive, defensive, and attacking strategies; decide which team member will present each specific point; practice presenting the points; and perform the debate in front of the class. A group grade will be given, based on how well the team members prepared and presented their points and how well they responded to the questions of the opposing team. The winning team will be determined by a vote of the audience. Debate team members will sit together facing their opponents with the class as the audience. (See Figure 1.)

Figure 1. THE LAYOUT OF THE DEBATE

The debaters are invited to speak by the debate monitor, who enforces strict time limits. (See Figure 2.)

Figure 2. ORDER OF THE DEBATE

Affirmative:	6 minutes for the affirmative side to construct its case
Both sides:	3 minutes for the negative side to cross-examine the affirmative side
Affirmative:	3 minutes for the audience to question the affirmative side
Negative:	6 minutes for the negative side to construct its case
Both sides:	3 minutes for the affirmative side to cross-examine the negative side
Negative:	3 minutes for the audience to question the negative side
BREAK:	2 minutes for each side to prepare its summary in private
Negative:	2 minutes for the negative side to present its summary
Affirmative:	2 minutes for the affirmative side to present its summary
Vote:	The audience writes either "Affirmative" or "Negative" on a piece of paper in response to the question: Which team presented its points and answered the questions in the clearest and most convincing way? Answers are collected, counted, and announced by the monitor.

Debaters may not speak when the opposing team is constructing or summarizing its case, but all debaters may speak at any time during the cross-examination. Strict time limits will be kept, ensuring that each debate will take 30 minutes. It is important that every member of the team participate and **contribute** to the preparation and the debate itself.

A. Form four groups by counting off by *4*s; students with the same number will be on the same team. (For example, all the *1*s are on one team.)

B. As a group choose one of the topics to debate. (See Figure 3.)

Figure 3. TOPICS FOR DEBATES

GROUP 1 TOPICS

- Gun Control: Although stricter gun control laws have been passed, such as **abolishing** the rights of citizens to own assault weapons, further laws should be passed and enforced to reduce crime in the United States.
- **Euthanasia:** Euthanasia should be legalized in the United States when a terminally ill patient in sound mind requests that a licensed doctor end his or her suffering.
- Your own idea and a specific change of policy related to it:

_____

_____

GROUP 2 TOPICS

- **Censorship** of TV Violence: Although TV violence has been regulated by new TV codes so that parents can better control what their children watch, further steps are needed to reduce the number of violent shows.
- Animals in Research: Animals should never be sacrificed for scientific research.
- Your own idea and a specific change of policy related to it:

_____

_____

GROUP 3 TOPICS

- Legalizing Drugs: Drugs should be legalized in the United States in order to reduce crime.
- Death Penalty: The death penalty should be enforced on all **inmates** in the United States convicted of committing a violent crime involving the loss of life.
- Your own idea and a specific change of policy related to it:

_____

_____

GROUP 4 TOPICS

- **Mandatory** AIDS Testing: All persons in the United States should be tested for AIDS annually if they are determined to be in a high-risk category.
- Equality of the Sexes: Men and women in the United States should have equal access to employment including service in the military and active combat.
- Your own idea and a specific change of policy related to it:

_____

_____

C. Divide the group equally to form the affirmative side and the negative side. If the group cannot decide within 5 minutes, the instructor will assign a topic and which members will be on each side.

D. Exchange names, and choose a leader whose job is to keep everyone involved, to keep the group on task, and to turn in the worksheet the day before the debates.

E. Either on your own or as a group, research the topic in the library in the same way you researched your speech topic. Copy at least two articles that have relevant information. Read them and highlight any useful information, making notes in the margins. Bring the articles to class.

F. Study the sample debate worksheet that Maria's group prepared. (See Figure 4 and Figure 5.)

Figure 4. Issues to Consider When Debating a Change in Policy

I.   Justification

    A.   Are there specific reasons to change things and not just leave them as they are?

    B.   Is the problem really important enough to justify a change?

II.   Plan

    A.   Is the plan workable?

    B.   Does the plan solve the problem?

III. Advantages

    A.   Does the plan produce advantages?

    B.   Do the advantages of the plan outweigh the disadvantages?

G. As a team, plan your offensive, defensive, and attacking strategies by filling out the worksheet together. Use correct outline form, and be sure your topics and subtopics are parallel and make sense. Show the worksheet to your instructor for comments. When the worksheet is approved, copy it for each member. The worksheet for you to use is on page 139.

H. Assign particular points and questions to each team member to ensure that everyone will speak up during the debate. (Refer to the "Useful Expressions" box at the end of the chapter if you need help. Notice that debaters use strong but polite language.)

I. Practice your part of the debate, and come to class with notes.

Figure 5. SAMPLE DEBATE WORKSHEET

SAMPLE DEBATE WORKSHEET

Position and Proposition

Affirmative. Abortion should be illegal in the United States.

OFFENSE

Our main points: Examples, proof, references:

I. Abortion is the taking
    of human life:
    A. The fetus is human.   Opposing Viewpoints: Abortion
    B. The fetus is alive.

II. Compare three options   CQ Researcher, Nov. 1993
    A. Aborting the child.
    B. keeping the child.
    C. Giving the child up for
        adoption.

DEFENSE

Weak points they may bring up: Our defense:

A fetus is not a child, so abortion   A fetus is human and it is alive,
   is not the taking of human life.   so abortion is the taking of human life.
Adoption can't solve all the problems,
   like
      — Dangers of illegal abortions.   — Compare the number of women dying
      — Cases of rape or incest.   to the number of aborted fetuses.
                                                    — There would be some exceptions.

ATTACK

Their probable points: Weaknesses in these points:

Policy would produce unwanted   There are waiting lists for couples
   children.   wanting to adopt. Children are wanted!
Policy would produce child abuse.   Abortion is the worst case of abuse.
Policy denies women control over   We all are denied the right to take
   their bodies.   the lives of others.

DEBATE WORKSHEET

Position and Proposition

OFFENSE

Our main points: Examples, proof, references:

DEFENSE

Weak points they may bring up: Our defense:

ATTACK

Their probable points: Weaknesses in these points:

▶ SPEAKING TASK

A. When the teams are ready to debate, select a timekeeper from the audience who will write in large size the numbers *3, 2, 1* and the word *Stop* on separate sheets of paper. She or he will time the debaters and will hold up the paper with the number *3* when the debater has only 3 minutes left to speak. The timekeeper will also signal the 2-minute and 1-minute marks and will raise the word *Stop* when the time has expired.

B. Select a monitor from the audience, who will introduce the debaters by name, read the proposition, invite each side to begin, interrupt the debate when time has expired, thank the participants, and collect and count the ballots.

C. Arrange the desks so team members sit next to each other and face their opponents with the class as the audience. Then begin the debate.

▶ POST-SPEAKING TASK

Discuss the debates as a class by answering these questions.

1. Which debate did you enjoy the most and why?
2. What were some of the more effective strategies used?
3. Did any of the debates make you change your mind about an issue? Which ones?
4. Were there any major points missing in any of the debates? Which points?

PHRASES FOR THE MONITOR

Welcome to our debate today on the proposition....

Representing the affirmative side are....

Thank you, Paul. Your time is up. And now the negative side has 3 minutes to....

PHRASES USED TO CONSTRUCT A CASE

There are three reasons why we need to change the policy regarding....

We have all seen the many problems caused by....

According to the September 23, 1998, edition of the *New York Times*, most women....

One article says that....

The most important fact is....

And now my teammate, Rosa, will present our second point....

PHRASES USED TO CROSS-EXAMINE

Maria, you said that.... But isn't it true that...?

You stated earlier, Rosa, that.... However, you didn't mention that....

If what you said about ... is true, then....

I'm not sure I understand your last point. Could you explain it again?

Just because ... is true, doesn't mean that ... is also true.

There could be another explanation for that. For example, ...

PHRASES USED TO ANSWER THE OPPOSITION

It may be true that.... But what about...?

Let me respond to that question by asking you...?

Although it is true that..., you can't forget that....

PHRASES USED TO SUMMARIZE

To summarize our points....

Although some may feel that..., research shows that....

CHAPTER 9

Writing a Commercial

▶ **THIEN: THE INTERNATIONAL STUDENTS' CLUB**

Thien has found friends and English speakers at a club activity. What clubs or other activities at your school provide opportunities to speak English?

Help with Vocabulary

Match the words and their definitions.

_ℓ_	1. **potluck**	a.	to reach, arrive, gain through effort
____	2. **keep on the lookout for**	b.	to take out, remove, get rid of, omit
____	3. **inadequacy**	c.	to be actively seeking
____	4. **put off**	d.	an Indian snack of potatoes, meat, and curry
____	5. **attain**	e.	a document listing one's educational and work experience
____	6. **samosa**	f.	to suggest ideas freely
____	7. **lift**	g.	short for "property"; things used in performing
____	8. **résumé**	h.	to postpone or delay doing something
____	9. **brainstorm**	i.	insufficiency, not being equal to what is required
____	10. **mention**	j.	to say a short statement that is not of great importance
____	11. **eliminate**	k.	a ride in someone's car
____	12. **prop**	l.	a type of party in which guests bring food to share

Write the correct vocabulary word from above and indicate its part of speech (verb (v.), noun (n.), adjective (adj.), adverb (adv.), or idiom) in each of the following sentences. Follow the example.

13. Why should you try to _____ your accent?

14. Can you give me a _____ to work? My car is being repaired.

15. _____ a gas station. I need to use the rest room.

16. The essay has more than one _____ ; it doesn't meet our standards.

17. You can _____ your goals if you are dedicated and persistent.

18. The _____ was so spicy that I needed water to wash it down.

19. It's a _____ potluck (adj.) _____ party, so I'm going to bring a fruit salad. What about you?

20. As the saying goes, "Don't _____ until tomorrow what you can do today."

21. We will _____ to find a solution to the problem.

22. This is not a real gun. It's just a _____ for the school play.

23. I need to rewrite my _____ now that I have completed my degree.

24. She _____ that the movie started at midnight.

Correct your answers by discussing them or by checking the Answer Key.

PART I: FOCUS ON LISTENING
Thien: The International Students' Club

- What do you notice about this sign-up sheet for the company's **potluck** picnic?
- Would you like to eat these foods for dinner?
- What are the advantages and disadvantages of having a potluck meal?

▶ **PRE-LISTENING TASK**

Overview: One of your goals is to be able to communicate effectively in English, which takes a lot of practice. Therefore, you must **keep on the lookout for** every opportunity to speak with others. Taking advantage of all those opportunities can be a challenge. Some people worry about their own **inadequacy** in speaking English, thinking, "What if people don't understand me?" or "What if I can't catch what they are saying?" It is important to remember that everyone makes plenty of mistakes when trying to master a new skill. You probably will be misunderstood, and you may misunderstand others. However, if you **put off** actively communicating in English on a daily basis, you may not **attain** your language-learning goals. In Chapter 1 you made a contract with yourself to seek more opportunities to speak English. Have you done that? Can you do more? In the following exercise you will listen to a situation in which Thien forced himself to communicate in English even though it was uncomfortable for him. When was the last time you challenged yourself to speak English outside this class?

A. Find a partner and answer the following questions.

1. Why is it important to take advantage of speaking opportunities?
2. Why is it difficult to do so?
3. What will happen if you put off actively communicating in English on a daily basis?
4. When was the last time you challenged yourself to speak English outside this class?
5. How are you doing on your contract from Chapter 1?

B. Discuss your answers as a class.

▶ LISTENING TASK 1

A. Listen to the conversation, and volunteer to tell the class where the conversation is taking place, who is involved, and what is happening.

B. Listen to the conversation again, and answer the multiple-choice questions that follow. Circle the best answer based on the information you hear.

1. How long have Abdul and Thien been at the party when the conversation begins?
   a. They have just gotten there.
   b. They have been there for a while.
   c. They have not gone to the party yet.

2. Before the party, Thien had probably told Abdul that
   a. he did not want to eat samosa.
   b. he couldn't bring any food to the party.
   c. he didn't want to go to the party.

3. The ISC stands for
   a. the International Students' Club.
   b. the Institute of South Carolina.
   c. the International Scholarship Committee.

4. When Eiko asks Thien to help her, he

    a. doesn't understand why.

    b. agrees to help.

    c. says she is good at art.

5. Eiko apologizes because

    a. she has asked for help.

    b. she forgot their names.

    c. she forgot to introduce Abdul and Thien to her friend.

6. Kyung Hee

    a. remembers Thien from a writing class.

    b. thought Mr. Winters gave a lot of writing assignments.

    c. dropped the writing class after a few weeks.

7. Abdul asks Thien

    a. if he can get a ride home with someone else.

    b. if he wants to leave early with him.

    c. Both a and b.

8. Eiko tells Thien that

    a. she could drive him home at 5 o'clock.

    b. Mrs. Adams would mind driving him home.

    c. he could get a lift home with her.

C. Correct your answers by discussing them or by checking the Answer Key.

▶ LISTENING TASK 2

A. With a partner, discuss the following questions.

1. What has helped you the most in your language-learning experience?
2. Has a book, a class, a school, or even joining a club helped you?
3. What is your secret to language learning?

📼 **B.** In the next section of this chapter, you and your group will plan and produce a short commercial like the one your are about to hear. Listen to the first half of Thien's commercial. As a class, answer the following questions.

1. What is being advertised?
2. What might the audience (ESL students) find funny?
3. What do you predict will happen in the next half of the commercial?

📼 **C.** Listen to the second half of the commercial. As a class, answer the following questions.

4. What important information is given about the club?
5. Besides learning English, what might be an extra benefit from going to the club?

D. Correct your answers by discussing them or by checking the Answer Key.

▶ **LISTENING TASK 3**

📼 **A.** Listen to another student-produced commercial, and be prepared to answer the following questions as a class.

1. What is being advertised?
2. What are the reasons someone should go there?
3. What aspect does the first graduate highlight?
4. What aspect does the second graduate highlight?
5. What aspect does the third graduate highlight?
6. Which commercial did you like better and why?

B. Correct your answers by discussing them or by checking the Answer Key.

PART II: FOCUS ON SPEAKING
Writing a Commercial

"That's Not My Job"

This is a story about four people named Everybody, Somebody, Anybody, and Nobody. There was an important job to be done, and Everybody was sure that Somebody would do it. Anybody could have done it, but Nobody did it. Somebody got angry about that, because it was Everybody's job. Everybody thought that Anybody could do it, but Nobody realized that Everybody wouldn't do it. It ended up that Everybody blamed Somebody when Nobody did what Anyone could have.

— Author unknown

What is the name of the person in this story who did what needed to be done? According to the story whose job was it? Who is the person who could have done it? Who is the person they thought would do it and in the end was blamed? What is the point of the story? Why do you think this story is included here in the text? (Refer to the "Useful Expressions" box at the end of the chapter to find polite ways to involve people in a conversation and polite ways to express disagreement.)

▶ **SPEAKING TASK**

Overview: You and your group will plan and produce a short commercial (from 1 to 5 minutes long) to advertise something that can help ESL students improve their English. You will perform the commercial live in front of the class. What you choose to advertise can be anything — a product, a service, a school, a book — anything you can think of, as long as it is something that will help your audience (ESL students) speak better English.

A. Working in groups of four or five, **brainstorm** about what you could advertise in your commercial. To brainstorm, **mention** any idea that comes to your mind. Offer one idea after another without stopping to evaluate any of them. Continue this process for a few minutes, jotting down the ideas quickly. The goal is to bring up as many ideas as possible.

B. Look over the ideas, and as a group take 10 minutes to discuss how you could develop them into a commercial. **Eliminate** the ideas that don't generate much enthusiasm. Develop a few of the ideas by considering what might take place in the commercial. Recall radio and TV commercials to discover more ideas.

C. After 10 minutes of discussion, decide on one idea and develop it further. Discuss which characters could be in the commercial, what each character could say and do, and how the commercial would end.

D. Discuss your ideas with the instructor, and get some feedback.

E. Write a script for the commercial so that it includes a part for every student in your group. (The script should be only a guide. It does not need to be memorized and should not be read when performing it for the class.) If you will perform the commercial on some later date, make a list of any **props** your group will need and who will bring them.

F. Practice the commercial, and perform it with enthusiasm when asked to present it to the class.

▶ **POST-SPEAKING TASK**

Overview: After viewing all the commercials made by the class, hold a lighthearted award ceremony like the Academy Awards. The class will nominate commercials in specific categories and then will vote for the winners.

A. Look at the following categories, and add some to the list. Write the list on the board.

Categories	*Nominees*	
Best Acting in Any Commercial	_____	_____
Worst Acting in Any Commercial	_____	_____
Funniest Commercial	_____	_____
Most Serious Commercial	_____	_____
Best Product Advertised	_____	_____
_____	_____	_____
_____	_____	_____
_____	_____	_____

B. Nominate two (and only two) commercials for each category by raising your hand and naming the category and commercial. (A commercial cannot be nominated by the students who wrote it.)

C. Write the name of each category on a ballot, and vote for the one commercial you think is the best in that category.

D. Collect the ballots and count the votes.

E. Present the awards with as much fanfare as you would like. Ask the winners to come to the front of the class for a handshake and to give a short acceptance speech.

Useful Expressions

WAYS TO TRY TO INVOLVE PEOPLE IN THE CONVERSATION

You haven't said much. How do you feel about what we have discussed so far?

I was wondering what you think about this?

What do you think about this?

Maybe _____ would like to tell us his thoughts about this.

Do you agree with what we've said?

Do you have any ideas?

POLITE WAYS TO EXPRESS DISAGREEMENT

I think that sounds good, but maybe we could … instead of.…

Those are good ideas. I was wondering if we could possibly consider.…

What would you think if we…?

CHAPTER 10

Talking about Different Cultures

▶ **EIKO: CULTURE CLASH, CULTURE BOOTHS**

Eiko and three other Japanese students are **hosting** a culture **booth** and explaining different aspects of Japanese culture to other students in the class. What aspects of your culture will you want to highlight in your culture booth?

Help with Vocabulary

Read each sentence. Write the number of the sentence that the **bold** word is in next to the definition. Then, after each definition, write the word and indicate its *part of speech* (verb (v.), noun (n.), adjective (adj.), preposition (prep.), adverb (adv.), or idiom). Follow the example.

1. I love to **host** parties at my new house.
2. I was told to go to the information **booth** and ask there.
3. I think that man behind you can **eavesdrop** on our conversation.
4. The dessert menu looks **tempting**, but I'm not going to ruin my diet.
5. She may have a **mood swing.** One minute she is happy, and the next she is depressed.
6. He was just here. He seemed to **disappear** when the police came.
7. After seeing that violent movie, I lost my **appetite.** I'll eat later.
8. I will **assume** he will pay for the meal since he invited us to dinner.
9. The **initial** plan was to meet in the park, but now we'll meet here.
10. Please **keep an eye on** my purse while I make a telephone call.
11. She wasn't prepared for the **ups and downs** of married life.
12. At first I thought I liked the idea, but now I **have second thoughts.**
13. Take advantage of the opportunity to study **abroad** and see the world.
14. She couldn't **cope** with the pressure, and she quit her job.
15. She was **hospitable** when we visited, offering food and wine.

____ a. a sudden, unexplained change in emotions _____

____ b. to watch or care for something or someone _____

____ c. beginning or original _____

_1_ d. to be responsible for giving a party or event _____ host (v.) _____

____ e. a place to give out information, or to have privacy _____

____ f. to deal with or handle _____

____ g. to listen to others without their knowledge or consent _____

____ h. a situation that causes one to want or do something _____

____ i. to reconsider a decision or have doubts about it _____

____ j. to suppose, to believe something is true when there is no proof _____

____ k. friendly or kind toward guests _____

____ l. high and low points, good and bad times _____

____ m. outside one's country _____

____ n. the desire to eat _____

____ o. to be removed from sight _____

Correct your answers by discussing them or by checking the Answer Key.

PART I: FOCUS ON LISTENING
Eiko: Culture Clash, Culture Booths

From *It's Still a Mom's Life* by David Sipress. Copyright © 1993 by David Sipress. Used by permission of Dutton Signet, a division of Penguin Books USA, Inc.

- What did this mother try to explain to her daughter?
- What do you think of the daughter's summary?
- Why does the mother look shocked?

One speaking project for this chapter requires you to explain and summarize a difficult topic, as this mother and daughter tried to do.

A. Eiko is home early from school, and she overhears Mrs. Adams on the phone. She soon realizes that the conversation is about her, and she listens in. She knows that it is rude to **eavesdrop,** but this is too **tempting.** She can't hear what the person on the phone is saying, but she can make some guesses. Listen to what Eiko hears. Then find a partner and discuss what you think the other person on the phone is saying, based on what Mrs. Adams says.

B. Discuss your answers as a class.

▶ LISTENING TASK

A. After listening to both sides of the telephone conversation, answer the following questions.

1. Why did Mrs. Adams call Patty Hernández?

   _____

   _____

2. What made Ms. Hernández assume that Eiko had been adjusting up until this point?

   _____

   _____

3. What things does Eiko do that worry Mrs. Adams?

   _____

   _____

4. What are Ms. Hernández' specific suggestions for Mrs. Adams?

   _____

   _____

B. Correct your answers by discussing them or by checking the Answer Key.

A. Patty Hernández, the counselor, told Mrs. Adams that it is normal for foreign students who study **abroad** to feel homesick and to **have second thoughts** about leaving their country. Form groups of three, and discuss ways to **cope** with such feelings.

B. As a group, discuss the following strategies and write down the advantages and disadvantages of each one.

1. When you are homesick or discouraged, the best thing is to write and send a letter home. (Consider the Chinese proverb "Never write a letter when you're angry.")

   Advantages:

   _____

   _____

   Disadvantages:

   _____

   _____

2. When you are homesick or discouraged, the best thing is to call home.

   Advantages:

   _____

   _____

   Disadvantages:

   _____

   _____

3. When you are homesick or discouraged, the best thing is to write in a diary.

   Advantages:

   _____

   _____

   Disadvantages:

   _____

   _____

4. When you are homesick or discouraged, the best thing is to talk about it with a friend or classmate.

Advantages:

_____

_____

Disadvantages:

_____

_____

5. When you are homesick or discouraged, the best thing is to make a list of all the reasons you came to this country, the good things that have happened, and the people you have met.

Advantages:

_____

_____

Disadvantages:

_____

_____

6. When you are homesick or discouraged, the best thing is to do something you love doing, like window shopping, walking on the beach, renting a video, and so on.

Advantages:

_____

_____

Disadvantages:

_____

_____

7. When you are homesick or discouraged, the best thing is to cry and feel sorry for yourself, thinking that you are all alone and that no one has ever felt as miserable as you.

Advantages:

_____

_____

Disadvantages:

_____

_____

8. When you are homesick or discouraged, the best thing is to _____

_____

9. When you are homesick or discouraged, the worst thing is to _____

_____

C. Select one student from your group to report to the class some of the points your group discussed.

D. Discuss the following Chinese poem. Why does the moon cause one to miss home?

> I raise my head
> to see the moon
> that shines outside
> my bedroom window.
> My head sinks down
> with heavy thoughts
> of my hometown
> so far away.

夜思

床前明月光
疑是地上霜
舉頭望明月
低頭思故鄉

李白

PART II: FOCUS ON SPEAKING
Talking about Different Cultures

▶ **PRE-SPEAKING TASK 1**

A. Form groups of three and discuss the following questions.

1. Which aspects of your native culture might people from other cultures find interesting? Which aspects might they find strange and hard to understand?
2. Which aspects of your native culture do you know something about? (Consider such areas as dress, food, religion, language, social interactions, greetings, education, work, home life, male and female roles, night life, government, children's stories.)
3. Which cultural events or activities did you most enjoy as a child? Why?

B. Discuss your answers with the entire class.

C. Select one aspect of your native culture that can be divided into a few clear categories or steps. For example, some cultural aspects that can be divided into categories are types of languages, religions, holidays, and ceremonies; some cultural aspects that can be divided into steps are preparing a dish, performing a ritual, preparing for a festival or holiday, and selecting a mate.

D. Write a brief outline that has three steps or three categories and a few supporting details. Do not write out the entire explanation, and do not use complete sentences.

E. Consider what examples and definitions you use to explain some aspects of your native culture. (Refer to the "Useful Expressions" boxes at the end of this and previous chapters.)

F. Read the steps in Speaking Task 1, and come to the next class ready to play three roles: the speaker, the listener, and the audience.

▶ **PRE-SPEAKING TASK 2**

A. Turn to the "Useful Expressions" box at the end of this chapter. Check off all the phrases you hear as you listen to a speaker explain the steps of a cultural event to a listener.

B. As a class, discuss which phrases you heard.

C. Listen to the speaker and the listener again, and fill in the first entry in the form on page 167.

D. Discuss your answers and evaluate the two students according to Step F in Speaking Task 1.

▶ SPEAKING TASK 1

A. To select random pairs, have a student draw a name from the "Speaker Envelope" and another name from the "Listener Envelope." Since both envelopes contain the names of every student, everyone will be both a speaker and a listener.

B. A student from the audience will act as a timekeeper. She or he will call "Time" for the speaker after 5 minutes, and for the listener after 3 minutes. The rest of the class takes notes, using the form "Notes for Speaking Task" on page 167.

C. The speaker and the listener sit in front of the class, facing each other. The speaker has up to 5 minutes to explain her or his topic to the listener.

D. The listener takes notes, gives feedback, and interrupts the speaker to ask for clarification. When the speaker has finished or when time is called, the listener has 3 minutes to summarize the speaker's explanation.

E. This process continues until every student has been both a speaker and a listener.

F. The <u>speaker</u> is graded on how well she or he:
   1. gives a clear, logical explanation
   2. provides appropriate examples, and definitions
   3. responds to the listener's questions and feedback

The <u>listener</u> is graded on how well she or he
   1. appears to be actively listening by giving feedback and paraphrasing
   2. interrupts the speaker for clarification or for more details
   3. summarizes the explanation

▶ POST-SPEAKING TASK 1

Take notes about each presentation, including the names of the speaker and listener, the topic, and the main idea. What did they do well, what could be improved? (What were the strong and weak points?) If your instructor does not give you copies of the form, copy it by hand on one side of a sheet of paper. The form for you to use is on page 167.

Overview: For this project you will get together with other students from your native country or culture and organize a culture booth. You will set up your booth in the classroom or activity room in order to introduce your classmates to your culture. To divide students into groups, your instructor will list all the countries represented in your class across the top of the chalkboard. The name of each student will then be written under the country from which he or she came. (If there are many students from a particular country, the group can be split by dividing the country into north and south, east and west. Ideally, each group will have four to six students. Some students may be the only representative of their country and may want to present by themselves. It may be possible to group countries together if they represent similar cultures. For example, Central American countries could be grouped together, if by doing so a group of four to six students would result. A total of six to eight groups is ideal. Two days may be needed for this project if the class is large or there are more than four groups.)

A. After the groups have been formed, meet with your group to decide which aspects of your culture you would like to present. Consider using the following props:

_____ 1. A large sign naming the country or countries you will present

_____ 2. A map of the world showing the location of your country

_____ 3. A map showing the country alone and parts of bordering countries

_____ 4. The flag of the country

_____ 5. Food that is traditional in the country

_____ 6. Traditional clothing

_____ 7. Traditional music and a tape or CD player

_____ 8. Photos showing the geography or special aspects of the country

_____ 9. Objects that represent various aspects of the culture

_____ 10. Posters to present the cultures, sports, major holidays and the like

B. Determine which students in your group will prepare the sign, map, food, and other props and which day you will host your booth. Every group member should be responsible for doing and bringing something. The day your group will host your booth is _____.

C. Ideally, an activity room should be acquired so that you can set up your booth on tables large enough for four students to sit or stand behind. On the day that you host your booth, come early if possible to set up your display. Remember to bring any supplies you will need, such as masking tape, a cassette player, plates, napkins, and so forth.

D. Present your booth to the class by having each member speak briefly about the various objects on display. Each group will be allotted 10 to 15 minutes.

E. After each group has presented its booth, the class may approach the booths to take a closer look, to ask questions, and to sample the food.

F. As classmates approach your booth, welcome them in your native language and in English, and offer them some food. Explain what the food is, and answer questions about the objects or posters at your booth. Act as though you are welcoming them into your home in your native country; be warm and **hospitable.**

G. As your classmates are eating, play music from all the countries presented, and teach each other to dance as you do in your native country.

▶ **POST-SPEAKING TASK 2**

A. Evaluate the culture booth experience by discussing the following questions.

1. What did you learn from this project about your native culture?
2. What did you learn about other cultures? Be specific.
3. Does knowing about other cultures help people to get along? How?

B. Consider the following statements. Then read Step C.

_____ 1. They are different from us. Let's run!

_____ 2. They are different from us. Let's change them to be like us.

_____ 3. They are different from us. Let's get rid of them!

_____ 4. They are different from us. Let's find out how and why.

_____ 5. They are different from us, but that is OK. Their way is just one of many ways to do things. Our way is also just one of many ways to do things.

_____ 6. They are different from us, but that is good. I am better off now with them than I was before without them.

C. What feelings lie behind each statement in Step B? Write one of the following words in the blank to the left of each statement.

fear	superiority	tolerance
acceptance	hatred	curiosity

D. Discuss the following questions as a class.

1. Which events in history might illustrate each statement?
2. Which statement illustrates the feelings of most people living in the city you live in?
3. Which statement sums up your own feelings?

LISTENER: ACTIVE FEEDBACK

AGREEMENT: Uh-HUH.
Mmm-HMMM.
Yes. Right.
Sure.
Exactly. I agree.
Definitely.

DOUBT: Oh, really?
Mmm—maybe.
Well,… hmm.
Oh?
You sure?

CONFUSION: What?
What was that last word?
I didn't get that last point.
Pardon?

UNDERSTANDING: Oh, now I get it.
Oh, I see.
So that's it.

CONTINUE: Go on.
And then?
What else?
Tell me more.
Please continue.

LISTENER: PARAPHRASING

I think what you are saying is that.…

If I understand you correctly, you say that.…

What you mean is that.…

In other words,…

Let me see if I understand correctly. There are three types of ___. Right?
And the first is.…

LISTENER OR SPEAKER: HESITATING

Mmmm.…

Well, let me think.…

How can I put it?

Let's see no,…

SPEAKER: REPHRASING

Well, What I meant to say was....

What I really meant was that....

Actually, I....

What I'm trying to say is....

SPEAKER: ASKING FOR A RESPONSE

Do you understand so far?

Was that clear?

Should I give you an example?

Any questions so far?

Would you like me to clarify anything?

Would you like me to define _____ ?

SPEAKER: RETURNING TO THE STORY

As I was saying,...

Going back to what I was saying earlier,...

To return to my second point,...

Where was I? Oh yes,...

NOTES FOR SPEAKING TASK

Names of students _____

Topic _____

Main idea _____

Strong points _____

Weak points _____

Names of students _____

Topic _____

Main idea _____

Strong points _____

Weak points _____

Names of students _____

Topic _____

Main idea _____

Strong points _____

Weak points _____

Names of students _____

Topic _____

Main idea _____

Strong points _____

Weak points _____

Names of students _____

Topic _____

Main idea _____

Strong points _____

Weak points _____

Vocabulary Review

MOTIVATION   initial   host

Euthanasia   Lottery

tempting   VERSUS

APPETITE   Booth

Enormous   OFFENSIVE

IMPROMPTU

brainstorm

potluck

ATTAIN

rapport   Samosa   lift

RÉSUMÉ

Confident

slip	adjacent	motivation	or else
lottery	fondest	cannot stand	enormous
impromptu	confident	stressed out	stand out

Fill in the blanks with the words from the box.

Like most teachers, I _____ (hate) grading
_____1_____

_____ (large) amounts of papers; however, one of my
_____2_____

_____ (favorite) memories of teaching grade school is of
_____3_____

reading the papers of one of my favorite students, Charlie. Charlie didn't

_____ (to be noticeable) in a crowd. He was neither handsome
_____4_____

nor outgoing and was not liked much by the girls and especially by the boys, who liked

to call him "Chicken-Out Charlie" because he would always run away from fights they

tried to pick with him. As a matter of fact, he was so shy that on the first day of class

when we used a _____ (random drawing) system to select
_____5_____

students to present a short _____ (without much preparation)
_____6_____

speech introducing themselves, he became so _____
_____7_____

(pressured or anxious) that he left the classroom and stayed in the boys' room until

the end of class. But give that boy a pencil, and watch out! He became a

_____ (sure, positive) young man who could touch the heart
_____8_____

of even the meanest classmate who teased him on the playground. Once, when it

seemed that the students' enthusiasm in a particular writing assignments was about to

_____ , (go down) and they needed some
_____9_____

_____ (encouragement), I read Charlie's paper to the class.
_____10_____

The class had never been so quiet. Two boys in the row _____
_____11_____

(near) to Charlie's glanced at each other with their mouths hanging open in amazement.

That day I told the students that they had better treat Charlie with respect,

_____ (words to introduce a threat) they might end up as
                    12

the bad guys in one of his best-selling novels! And from that day on, "Chicken-Out Charlie"

was just called Charlie, and sometimes even Chuck.

biased	inaccurate	refute	anecdote
deterrent	allot	relevant	controversial
stand in awe	rapport	proposition	persuade

Fill in the blanks with the words from the box.

Journal Entry 26

I'll never forget today and the feeling of victory. I have been elected the student-body president, and my best friends were elected vice-president, treasurer, and secretary. The debate last week is what helped us. We were able to _____ 1 (convince) the entire audience to vote for us. Mike was great. The teacher could only _____ 2 (give) 2 minutes to him to speak about the _____ 3 (debatable) _____ 4 (proposal) that our school should accept a strict dress code, forcing us all to wear uniforms. We had done our homework on this issue, and we knew that the majority of students did not want a dress code. Surveys had shown that having a dress code would not improve students' grades or behavior. The students we were debating, however, had not done their homework. They just told a funny _____ 5 (entertaining story) or two that was not _____ 6 (related) to the issue, and they read from _____ 7 (prejudiced) articles about the advantages of having a dress code. Then Mike stepped up to the podium and very clearly and convincingly stated that a dress code would not be a _____ 8 (hindrance) to bad behavior. He was able to _____ 9 (prove wrong) their arguments by stating that their information was _____ 10 (not correct) and outdated.

He had such _____ (a good relationship) with the audience
                              11

that everyone stood up to cheer when he had finished: a standing ovation! I even

saw our English teacher _____ of Mike. Now that was an
                                        12

accomplishment! Maybe after we graduate, we'll move on to Washington, D.C.

abolish	censorship	construct	contribute	mandatory
defensive	euthanasia	fetus	inmate	
offensive	sacrifice	versus	cross-examine	

Fill in the blanks with the words from the box.

The politician was very clear about how he felt regarding several controversial issues related to life and death. Regarding abortion, he wanted to reverse the 1973 Supreme Court ruling on Roe _____ (against) Wade. He felt that

$_1$

a _____ (unborn child) had the right to life. He said "We cannot

$_2$

_____ (give up) the life of any unborn child unless the mother's

$_3$

life is in danger." On the issue of _____ (causing death painlessly),

$_4$

he also believed in saving life rather than ending it. When reporters began to

_____ (question closely) him, he said, "I will never support a law

$_5$

that allows doctors to _____ (jointly participate in) to the death of a

$_6$

patient. A doctor's purpose is to save and preserve life, not end it." When asked about

the death penalty, he said that he opposed the _____ (required)

$_7$

death sentence for an _____ (prisoner) convicted of a violent crime

$_8$

that involved the loss of life. He wanted to _____ (end completely)

$_9$

the death penalty. He felt that the government should take an _____

$_{10}$

(attacking) strategy to fight crime rather than taking a _____

$_{11}$

(defending) strategy. For example, he supported the _____

$_{12}$

(examining and removing objectionable content) of TV violence, and he wanted to

_____ (build) federal programs that teach people skills so that
13

they can get jobs. He felt that would reduce crime. In summary, he said, "I will seek to

protect life in any form, from the unborn child to the suffering patient and the prison

inmate. Life is too valuable to be taken by society."

attain	brainstorm	eliminate	inadequacy
lift	mention	potluck	put off
prop	keep on the lookout for	samosa	résumé

Fill in the blanks with the words from the box.

MARY: Hello, Sue. Have you decided what you're making for the _____

1

(type of party in which guests bring food to share) party this weekend?

SUE: Hi, Mary. Well, I may make _____ (a type of Indian food).

2

How about you?

MARY: I don't know yet. Got any ideas? I have had to _____ (postpone)

3

thinking about it because I've been so busy making the main

_____ (object used in performing) for the school play. To tell

4

you the truth, if I don't find a ride, I may not even go to the party.

SUE: I can give you a _____ (a ride in a car).

5

MARY: Great! Thank you, Sue. Say, how is your job hunt going? Have you had any luck?

SUE: No. It isn't easy to I think I need to write a more effective _____

6

(document listing one's background and experience). I haven't even been

invited for an interview yet.

MARY: I saw a great book on résumé writing. I can't recall the title, but I think it's called

" _____ (gain through effort) Your Goals!" I will

7

_____ (actively seek) a good "how to" book with a lot of

8

sample résumés and tips on what to include.

SUE: As a matter of fact, I have a résumé-writing book already. It says a good way to

begin is to _____ (suggest ideas or solutions), writing down

9

anything and everything that comes to mind, such as clubs I've attended and

awards I've received. Then it said to _____ (remove) all the

                                             10

things that may draw attention to any _____ (insufficiency,

                                           11

weak areas) I might have.

MARY: You should also _____ (talk about) your strengths, such as

                                           12

being bilingual and your experiences living in other countries.

SUE: I didn't think of that. Good idea, Mary, I'll include it.

MARY: Now that I've given you an idea for your résumé, how about giving me one

for the potluck party? What should I make?

SUE: Why don't you just help me make my samosa. You can come over to my place

the afternoon of the party. And if there's time left, you can help me with my

résumé too!

MARY: Sounds great!

host	eavesdrop	disappear	keep an eye on
appetite	initial	abroad	cope
assumed	mood swing	hospitable	tempting
have second thoughts	booth	ups and downs	

Fill in the blanks with the words from the box.

Dear Jill,

Thanks for your note. Yes, I'm going to the basketball game; and no, I don't think Richie Alexander is cute. Have you lost your mind, girl? But wait until you hear my new gossip! Between classes, I was in the girls' room and was able to _____ (listen to secretly) on Loretta and ₁
Roxanne! I know it wasn't nice, but it was too _____ ₂
(a situation that makes you do something you should not do). Roxanne walked in and went straight to the mirror, of course, to put on her makeup for the tenth time. And Loretta went into the _____ (a ₃
place for privacy) next to mine to get toilet paper because she's crying her eyes out — another _____ (sudden change in ₄
emotion). Anyway, Loretta said that last weekend Eddie, her boyfriend — you know that cute guy in our math class — was going to _____ ₅
(give) a party. She _____ (suppose) that she ₆
had been invited, and she showed up around 9 o'clock to find Eddie with this cute new girl from _____ (outside ₇
one's country) — some European country. Anyway, Loretta couldn't _____ (handle) with watching them together, ₈

so she made herself _____ (remove from sight).

But before she left the party, she asked a friend to _____

(watch) them for her. She found out that Eddie was very

_____ (friendly) to this new girl and that they

danced most of the night. When Loretta finished this story, she started

crying again and said she hadn't eaten in two days and had lost her

_____ (desire to eat). Hey, Jill, maybe she'll

finally lose weight. Ha, ha! So then Roxanne tried to comfort Loretta, saying,

"All relationships have their _____ (good and

bad times). Don't worry, Loretta. I heard that Eddie's _____

(beginning) plan was to invite you to his party. But then he began to

_____ (reconsider, change his mind) when he

saw you talking with Richie Alexander. He got mad and invited that new girl

just to make you jealous. So see, he really does love you." Can you believe it,

Jill? They think he still likes her? If he loves her so much why was he dancing

with Miss Europe? The best part was that Roxanne and Loretta never even

knew I was listening. Got to go, Jill. Math class is almost over. Write back!

Christine

Class Evaluation Form

CLASS EVALUATION FORM

Do *not* put your name on this paper! Please answer honestly.

Circle the appropriate answer.

Contract	Great	Good	OK	Poor	Bad
Tape	Great	Good	OK	Poor	Bad
Survey	Great	Good	OK	Poor	Bad
Movie Review	Great	Good	OK	Poor	Bad
Interview	Great	Good	OK	Poor	Bad
Impromptu Speech	Great	Good	OK	Poor	Bad
Prepared Speech	Great	Good	OK	Poor	Bad
Debate	Great	Good	OK	Poor	Bad
Commercial	Great	Good	OK	Poor	Bad
Cultural Summary	Great	Good	OK	Poor	Bad
Culture Booth	Great	Good	OK	Poor	Bad
Quizzes, Tests	Great	Good	OK	Poor	Bad

Circle the appropriate answer.

1. I would recommend this *class* to my friends.	Yes	Maybe	No
2. I would recommend this *teacher* to my friends.	Yes	Maybe	No
3. I would recommend this *book* to my friends.	Yes	Maybe	No
4. I felt comfortable with my *classmates.*	Yes	Maybe	No
5. I can *understand and speak* English better now.	Yes	Maybe	No
6. There were *enough homework* and projects.	Yes	Maybe	No
7. There were *too much homework* and projects.	Yes	Maybe	No

Finish each of the following sentences.

1. The best part of this class was _____

2. The worst part of this class was _____

3. This class could be improved by doing more_____

4. This class could be improved by doing less _____

5. I would like to say that _____

_____

Glossary

Abolish   to destroy, to do away with, to end completely (v.). I wish we could **abolish** all forms of child abuse. Ch. 8

Abroad   outside one's country (adv.). Take advantage of the opportunity to study **abroad** and see the world. Ch. 10

Adjacent   near, close by (adj.). Write your name in the first column and your child's name in the **adjacent** column. Ch. 6

Adopt   to take in (v.). Although I understand his views, I can't **adopt** them as my own. Ch. 5

Advantage   a benefit, good point (n.). One **advantage** of living outside the city is breathing fresh air. Ch. 2

Allot   to give, set aside for (v.). She will **allot** only 10 minutes for each student's oral report. Ch. 7

Analogy   a comparison of two things in order to explain a point (n.). In that **analogy,** people are ingredients, and society is soup. Ch. 5

Anecdote   a short, entertaining story (n.). She has a favorite **anecdote** about her children. Ch. 7

Anxious   worried, afraid (adj.). Before I take tests, I get **anxious** and bite my nails. Ch. 1

Appetite   the desire to eat (n.). After seeing that violent movie, I lost my **appetite.** I'll eat later. Ch. 10

As a matter of fact   introduces an example or information (idiom). I like his music. **As a matter of fact,** I have most of his CDs. Ch. 3

Assume   to suppose, to believe something is true when there is no proof (v.). I will **assume** he will pay for the meal since he invited us to dinner. Ch. 10

Attain   to reach, arrive, gain through effort (v.). You can **attain** your goals if you are dedicated and persistent. Ch. 9

Axis   a line on which things are drawn symmetrically (n.). The line across the bottom of the graph is the horizontal **axis.** Ch. 5

Biased   prejudiced, in favor or against someone (adj.). He is **biased.** He gave the award to his own students, but we deserved it. Ch. 7

Booth   a place to give out information, or for privacy (n.). I was told to go to the information **booth** and ask there. Ch. 10

Brainstorm   to suggest ideas freely (v.). We will **brainstorm** to find a solution to the problem. Ch. 9

Cannot stand   to hate, intensely dislike (v., idiom). I **cannot stand** it when you tell me how to drive. Keep quiet, or take a bus. Ch. 6

Celebrate   to have a good time in honor of an achievement (v.). Let's **celebrate** after graduation by having a party at my house! Ch. 5

Censorship   a means of examining things to remove objectionable content (n.). We feel **censorship** of TV is needed in order to reduce violence. Ch. 8

Challenge   to dare to confront, to urge or provoke (v.). The football players may not like it, but the coach is right to **challenge** them. Ch. 2

Cheer up   to make someone who is sad feel better (v., idiom). My child's smile can **cheer** me **up** when I come home from a hard day. Ch. 5

Chicken out   to not do something because one is afraid (v., idiom). She may **chicken out** and not take the class with the strict instructor. Ch. 1

Clarification   an explanation used to make something clear (n.). He was confused about the directions and asked for **clarification.** Ch. 2

Concern   problem, worry (n.). I have a **concern** about the party, and I need to discuss it with you. Ch. 4

Confident   sure, positive, certain (adj.). She was so **confident** in what she was saying that I believed her. Ch. 6

Consistency   firmness or thickness of a liquid (n.). Add flour to the soup to give it a thicker **consistency.** Ch. 5

Construct   to plan, to make, to build (v.). Let's **construct** a program to help foreign students find jobs. Ch. 8

Contribute   to give jointly with a group of others (v.). She didn't **contribute** money for the ticket, so she doesn't get a share of the prize. Ch. 8

Controversial   debatable, having opposing sides (adj.). They will debate a **controversial** subject like abortion or gun control. Ch. 7

Cope   to deal with or handle (v.). She couldn't **cope** with the pressure, and she quit her job. Ch. 10

Cover the cost   to be enough to pay for (v., idiom). My paycheck does not even **cover the cost** of my tuition this semester. Ch. 3

Cross-examine   to question closely to find out the truth (v.). When the prosecution was able to **cross-examine** her, the woman admitted she had killed them. Ch. 8

Dedicated   devoted to (adj.). She is so **dedicated** to her new job that she even worked on Christmas. Ch. 4

Defensive   the side of a team that defends the goal or position (adj.). The **defensive** side should prevent the other team from scoring any points. Ch. 8

Demanding   requiring a lot of (adj.). My boss is too **demanding.** I can never please him. Ch. 1

Deterrent   a hindrance, something that prevents or stops something else (n.). Some people feel the death penalty is not a **deterrent** for crime. Ch. 7

Disadvantage   inconvenience, hindrance, bad point (n.). One **disadvantage** of living in the city is polluted air. Ch. 2

Disappear   to be removed from sight (v.). He was just here. He seemed to **disappear** when the police came. Ch. 10

Discouraged   sad, troubled, depressed (adj.). I am **discouraged** about my grades. I don't think I will pass the class. Ch. 4

Eavesdrop   to listen to others without their knowledge or consent (v.). I think that man behind you can **eavesdrop** on our conversation. Ch. 10

Eliminate   to take out, to remove, to get rid of, to omit (v.). Why should you try to **eliminate** your accent? Ch. 9

Embarrassed   ashamed, humiliated (adj.). When I get **embarrassed,** my cheeks turn bright red. Ch. 1

Encourage   to cheer up, to comfort, to assure (v.). She will **encourage** me to try again. She said many people fail the first time. Ch. 4

End up   to result in (v.). If you don't study, you may **end up** with a bad grade. Ch. 2

Enormous   very big, large (adj.). Whenever I get anxious, I get an **enormous** appetite and eat anything in sight. Ch. 6

Enthusiastic   able to create interest or excitement (adj.). She is an **enthusiastic** teacher who can excite her students. Ch. 2

Entrepreneur   a person who organizes and manages a business (n.). His dream is not to work for anyone and to become an **entrepreneur.** Ch. 1

Euthanasia   the act or method of causing death painlessly (n.). She was in pain and dying, so the family sadly agreed on **euthanasia.** Ch. 8

Feedback   input, information (n.). Listen to my speech, and give me some **feedback.** How can I improve the speech? Ch. 2

Fetus   in humans, the unborn young from the end of the third month to birth (n.). An unborn child is called a **fetus** from the end of the third month until birth. Ch. 8

Fit in   to sense or have a feeling of belonging (v., idiom). Everyone I know is married with children. As a single guy, I don't **fit in.** Ch. 4

Fondest   favorite, most cherished (adj.). My **fondest** memory is of my grandmother brushing my hair. Ch. 6

From time to time   at different times, every so often (idiom). The instructor said that she would call the student **from time to time.** Ch. 3

Frustrate   to disappoint (v.). It can **frustrate** me when I know what to say but I can't say it in English. Ch. 1

Get down for a nap   to try to get a child to sleep a short time during the day (v., idiom). It is hard to **get** the baby **down for a nap** with the TV on. Ch. 1

Glance   to look at something quickly (v.). I didn't get a good look at him. I only **glanced** at him for a moment. Ch. 2

GPA   the grade-point average of all one's grades. (n.). He got straight A's in high school, a perfect 4.0 **GPA.** Ch. 1

Hang in there   to not give up; to persevere, to continue, to carry on (v., idiom). I know this is a hard class for you, but **hang in there.** It will get easier. Ch. 4

Have second thoughts   to reconsider a decision or have doubts (v., idiom). At first I thought I liked the idea, but now I **have second thoughts.** Ch. 10

Hectic   busy, frantic, disordered (adj.). I've had a **hectic** day. I was so busy that I didn't have a minute to sit down. Ch. 3

Help myself   to serve yourself (v., idiom). I will **help myself** to some coffee and wait for the meeting to begin. Ch. 5

Hinder   to make difficult, to block or obstruct (v.). Working so many hours can **hinder** his ability to get good grades. Ch. 2

Hold down a job   to be able to keep a job (v., idiom). To **hold down a job** while being a full-time student is challenging. Ch. 3

Homestay   a program that houses foreign students with native families (adj.). She is in the **homestay** program offered by the university. Ch. 5

Horizontal   from left to right or side to side (adj.). The **horizontal** stripes on his shirt make him look muscular. Ch. 5

Hospitable   friendly or kind toward guests (adj.). She was **hospitable** when we visited, offering food and wine. Ch. 10

Host   to be responsible for giving a party or event (v.). I love to **host** parties at my new house. Ch. 10

Impromptu   without much preparation, spontaneous (adj.). His **impromptu** speech was so good that many people thought it had been prepared. Ch. 6

Inaccurate   not correct (adj.). The newspaper printed **inaccurate** information. The dates were wrong. Ch. 7

Inadequacy   insufficiency, not being equal to what is required (n.). The essay has more than one **inadequacy;** it doesn't meet our standards. Ch. 9

Initial   beginning or original (adj.). The **initial** plan was to meet in the park, but now we'll meet here. Ch. 10

Inmate   a person who is being held in jail or an institution (n.). The **inmate** told the prison guard that he was sorry for what he had done. Ch. 8

Interrupt   to break off, to cause someone to stop (v.). Children need to be taught not to **interrupt** adults who are talking. Ch. 2

Jot down   to write down quickly (v., idiom). Let me **jot down** your phone number in my address book. Ch. 1

Just the fact that   introduces evidence or proof (idiom). **Just the fact that** he called you tells you that he is thinking of you. Ch. 4

Keep an eye on   to watch or care for something or someone (v., idiom). Please **keep an eye on** my purse while I make a telephone call. Ch. 10

Keep on the lookout for   to be actively seeking (v., idiom). **Keep on the lookout for** a gas station. I need to use the rest room. Ch. 9

Keep track of   to keep a record of, to remember (v., idiom). I should **keep track of** all the money I spend by eating out. Ch. 1

Kind of   to a little degree, slightly, not very much (adv., idiom). I **kind of** like him, but I'm not sure if he likes me, so don't say anything. Ch. 3

Leftovers   prepared food that has not been consumed and is saved (n.). I don't feel like cooking. Let's eat some **leftovers.** Ch. 5

Lift   a ride in someone's car (n.). Can you give me a **lift** to work? My car is being repaired. Ch. 9

Lottery   a system to select a winner by random drawing (n.). I usually do not gamble, but I like to play the **lottery** now and then. Ch. 6

Mandatory   required, something that must be done (adj.). It is **mandatory** to wear seat belts in cars. It's not an option any longer. Ch. 8

Mention   to say a short statement that is not of great importance (v.). She **mentioned** that the movie started at midnight. Ch. 9

Mood swing   a sudden, unexplained change in emotions (n.). She may have a **mood swing.** One minute she is happy and the next she is depressed. Ch. 10

Motivation   encouragement, reasons for taking an action (n.). Her **motivation** for coming here was to get a better education. Ch. 6

Negotiate   to bargain (v.). The president would not **negotiate** on that point at all. Ch. 5

Offensive   the side of a team that must score points or attack (adj.). The **offensive** side of the basketball team is responsible for scoring points. Ch. 8

Or else   introduces a threat or alternative (idiom). You either say you are sorry, **or else** I'll leave you. Ch. 6

Persuade   to convince, to talk into (v.). I could not **persuade** my mother to let me go on the trip to California. Ch. 7

Potluck   a type of party in which guests bring food to share (adj.). It's a **potluck** party, so I'm going to bring a fruit salad. What about you? Ch. 9

Pretty   somewhat, very (adv.). You did **pretty** well. You should be proud of yourself. Ch. 3

Probation   a period of testing that will determine one's outcome (n.). Because of her poor grades, she is on academic **probation.** Ch. 1

Prop   short for "property"; things used in performing (n.). This is not a real gun. It's just a **prop** for the school play. Ch. 9

Proposition   something offered for consideration, a subject to be discussed (n.). His **proposition** is not clearly stated. Is he for abortion or against it? Ch. 7

Put off   to postpone or delay doing something (v., idiom). As the saying goes, "Don't **put off** till tomorrow what you can do today." Ch. 9

Rapport   a close relationship, agreement, harmony (n.). He has established **rapport** with his students. They listen to his every word. Ch. 7

Reasonable   fair, right, sensible, rational (adj.). The house is not too expensive. As a matter of fact, the price is very **reasonable.** Ch. 4

Refute   to prove to be wrong (v.). He did not even try to **refute** the strong arguments made by the lawyer. Ch. 7

Relevant   having to do with, relating to (adj.). A **relevant** subject to discuss with teenagers is the danger of drug abuse. Ch. 7

Résumé   a document listing one's educational and work experience (n.). I need to rewrite my **résumé** now that I have completed my degree. Ch. 9

Sacrifice   to give up something of value in order to achieve something else (v.). They **sacrifice** their free time on the weekends to help the homeless. Ch. 8

Samosa   an Indian snack of potatoes, meat, and curry (n.). The **samosa** was so spicy that I needed water to wash it down. Ch. 9

Shift   a period of time at work (n.). I work the night **shift** and don't get home until 6 A.M. Ch. 1

Slip   to go down (v.). A student's grades may **slip** during periods of stress. Ch. 6

Sponsor   to support a person financially (v.). He agreed to **sponsor** me in the United States. He will pay for my rent and tuition. Ch. 3

Stand in awe   to be amazed, in wonder with fear and respect (v.). The hikers **stand in awe** before the beauty of the mountains. Ch. 7

Stand out   to be noticeably different (v., idiom). His blonde hair made him **stand out** among his Asian classmates. Ch. 6

Strategy   a plan or tactic (n.). What is a good **strategy** for test taking? Ch. 2

Stressed out   feeling the effects of pressure or stress (adj., idiom). You seem **stressed out** by your problems at work. Why not take a vacation? Ch. 6

Strict   enforces rules severely (adj.). His parents are very **strict.** He cannot go out on weeknights. Ch. 1

Suicide   **to kill oneself, or if used idiomatically,** to do something difficult or dangerous intentionally (n.). Working three part-time jobs is **suicide!** Don't work so hard. Ch. 1

Survey   a questionnaire used to learn people's opinions (n.). They did a **survey** to see how many people drive after drinking. Ch. 3

Take advantage of   to use to one's own benefit (v., idiom). You should **take advantage of** his office hours and get help. Ch. 4

Take seriously   to act in a way that shows something is important (v., idiom). You must **take** this **seriously**. One more *D* and you will fail the class. Ch. 4

Tearjerker   a movie that makes you want to cry (n.). That movie was a real **tearjerker.** I used up a whole box of tissue. Ch. 4

Tempting   a situation that causes one to want or do something (adj.). The dessert menu looks **tempting,** but I'm not going to ruin my diet. Ch. 10

Tolerance   the ability to endure, to accept but not share (n.). I have developed **tolerance** for his smoking. It doesn't bother me as much now. Ch. 4

Tragic   terrible, sad, unfortunate (adj.). She made a **tragic** mistake and let her child out of the car seat. Ch. 5

Typical   usual, common (adj.). A **typical** workday for me begins at 8 A.M and ends at 5 P.M. Ch. 3

UCLA   University of California at Los Angeles (n.). Her daughter goes to **UCLA** and majors in Political Science. Ch. 5

Ups and downs   high and low points, good and bad times (n., idiom). She wasn't prepared for the **ups and downs** of married life. Ch. 10

Versus   in contest against (prep.). The 1973 Supreme Court ruling on Roe **versus** Wade made abortion legal in the United States. Ch. 8

Vertical   upright, straight up and down (adj.). The **vertical** blinds you put on the windows look great. Ch. 5

Workload   the amount of work one has to do (n.). He has a heavy **workload.** I doubt if he'll have time to help us. Ch. 3

APPENDIX C

Answer Key

CHAPTER 1

Help with Vocabulary — *Page 2*

9	a.	the grade-point average of all one's grades	GPA (n.)
5	b.	a person who organizes and manages a business	entrepreneur (n.)
12	c.	ashamed, humiliated	embarrassed (adj.)
3	d.	to disappoint	frustrate (v.)
10	e.	a period of testing that will determine one's outcome	probation (n.)
8	f.	a period of time at work	shift (n.)
1	g.	worried, afraid	anxious (adj.)
14	h.	to kill oneself, or if used idiomatically, to do something difficult or dangerous intentionally	suicide (n.)
2	i.	to write down quickly	jot down (v.)
11	j.	to try to get a child to sleep a short time during the day	get down for a nap (v.)
13	k.	requiring a lot of	demanding (adj.)
6	l.	enforces rules severely	strict (adj.)
4	m.	to keep a record of, to remember	keep track of (v.)
7	n.	to not do something because one is afraid	chicken out (v.)

Tapescript for Listening Task 1A — *Pages 4–5*

ABDUL: What a line! Even if I do get all my classes, I don't know if I will be able to stay in them if my work schedule changes. Working forty hours a week and taking 12 units is **suicide.** What if I can't keep up with the homework or I'm asked to work overtime at work? I hope I get an easy teacher. I heard that Miller is **demanding** and **strict,** making you do movie reviews, debates, and interviews and lowering your grade after only four absences. I hope Miller isn't the only choice left by the time I register. This line better get moving, or I'll be late for my afternoon **shift.** It was a lot simpler back home. There, students don't have to work to survive.

EIKO: I hope I do well in my classes. If I don't get a high enough **GPA,** I will lose my chance to study here. Maybe Cindy, the girl I live with in the United States, will help me with my homework. She is always so busy with her boyfriends though. I bet everyone in the class has lived here for years and speaks like a native. I hope there will be some other Japanese students in the class. If I find out we have to do any speeches, I'll **chicken out** and take a reading class. Maybe I can take a Japanese class; that would be an easy *A.* Why didn't I pay attention in my English classes in elementary school in Japan? What if I don't understand what the teacher says and am too **embarrassed** to ask her to repeat? What if I fail and am sent back to Japan without a degree? What time is it in Japan now? I wonder what my friends are doing.

MARIA: I am so **frustrated!** What am I doing here? I must be the oldest one in line. Some of these kids look as though they should be in junior high school. Maybe the classes are already full, and I won't be able to get in. I probably can't afford it anyway. Someone said that the fees went up again. That can't be true. They went up last semester. I wonder what the books will cost. I hope the kids are OK at my brother's house. He'll never get José **down for a nap** with all those other kids there. Maybe I will have time to pick up some meat for dinner before I pick them up. By the looks of this line, I'll be here for dinner. Oh my. I have so many things to worry about, it is almost impossible to **keep track of** them all.

THIEN: I'm so anxious about my grades. I hope I get an easy teacher. I can't fail this class again. Being on **probation,** if I fail, I'm out; and then I'll never learn how to speak English. I can't get a job if I can't speak English. Sometimes I hate English. I'll never be able to speak and understand it as I do Vietnamese. Maybe I'll just live in Little Saigon and be a waiter speaking Vietnamese. A waiter? I came all this way to be a waiter? No. I want a better job. Yeah, I want to run my own place, to be my own boss, an **entrepreneur.** I'll have twenty guys working for me. Sure! That is, if I ever get through this registration line.

Answers for Listening Task 2A — *Pages 5–7*

ABDUL: 1. classes,   2. work,   3. 40,   4. suicide,   5. overtime,
6. demanding,   7. strict,   8. lowering,   9. choice,   10. shift,
11. survive

EIKO: 1. well,   2. GPA,   3. help,   4. busy,   5. everyone,   6. native,
7. Japanese,   8. chicken out,   9. easy,   10. attention,
11. embarrassed,   12. fail,   13. degree,   14. friends

MARIA: 1. frustrated,   2. oldest,   3. kids,   4. full,   5. afford,   6. fees,
7. books,   8. down for a nap,   9. dinner,   10. worry,
11. keep track of

THIEN: 1. anxious,   2. probation,   3. job,   4. hate,   5. Vietnamese,
6. waiter,   7. run,   8. entrepreneur,   9. registration

CHAPTER 2

Help with Vocabulary — *Page 14*

9	a. an explanation used to make something clear	clarification (n.)
3	b. a benefit, good point	advantage (n.)
6	c. input, information	feedback (n.)
1	d. to make difficult, to block or obstruct	hinder (v.)
7	e. to dare to confront, to urge or provoke	challenge (v.)
5	f. to break off, to cause someone to stop	interrupt (v.)
11	g. to look quickly at something	glance (v.)
2	h. a plan or tactic	strategy (n.)
8	i. to result in	end up (v.)
10	j. able to create interest or excitement	enthusiastic (adj.)
4	k. inconvenience, hindrance, bad point	disadvantage (n.)

Answers for Pre-Listening Task 2A — *Page 16*

The best answer is number 4. Numbers 1 and 2 cause a student to miss the next part of the lecture. Numbers 3 and 7 are too passive, and most likely a student will not get the question answered. Numbers 5 and 8 are not bad, but the teacher could leave right after class, and the classmate could be wrong. Number 6 takes a lot of time and effort; however, listening again to the tape could be helpful.

Answers for Pre-Listening Task 2D — *Page 16*

1. T, 2. T, 3. F, 4. T, 5. F (*Note:* Some teachers do not like to be interrupted at all. Be sure to be polite. If you notice that your question disturbs the teacher, then use another strategy next time.)

Tapescript for Listening Tasks 1A and 1B — *Page 17*

MRS. WOODS: Your first project for this class, the monologue tape, is due next week. It's called *a monologue* because only one person is speaking. The topic I want you to speak about is yourself; it's a self-introduction. After a greeting like, "Hello, Mrs. Woods," tell me your name and native country, and describe what you will be discussing. Then move on to your main points, which are your family and native country, the reasons you came to the United States, your current situation, your hopes for the future, and, in conclusion, the reason you are taking this class. There are three requirements. First, the tape must be clear. That means little or no background noise, clear pronunciation, and a nice loud speaking voice. I must be able to hear you! You may have music from your native country playing softly in the background if you wish. However, remember that your voice must be loud and clear. Second, make sure the tape is the correct length: at least 5 minutes but less than 10 minutes. Time the tape when you finish, because a tape that is less than 5 minutes will receive a lower grade. Finally, make sure to speak freely from an outline. *Do not* read a written text. That sounds very boring, and you should practice speaking naturally, not reading. To repeat the three requirements: The tape must be clear, between 5 and 10 minutes long, and sound natural, not read.

Now, let me give you some suggestions about how to prepare. First, I suggest that you review the grading criteria for this project, as shown on the form. We will go over the form together, soon. Next, complete the outline, writing a few words and phrases, not entire sentences. Record yourself speaking freely from your outline. Listen to your tape and grade it as though you are the teacher. Finally, re-record the tape, and try to improve it.

Now, let's look at the grading criteria. You will be graded on three areas: content, presentation, and mechanics. For content, I will ask: Did you stay on topic? Were you well organized? Was your monologue interesting? The questions I ask for the presentation grade are: Was the tape loud and clear? Did you sound **enthusiastic?** Was your monologue well practiced, but not read? And were your pronunciation and grammar good? About mechanics I ask: Did you follow directions? Was the tape the correct length? Was it rewound? Was the tape labeled with your name and turned in by the due date? That's it.

The monologue tape does require a lot of time and effort, but it gives you speaking practice. Moreover, it helps me get to know you and your language skills. I hope you enjoy making the tape. Are there any questions?

Answers for Listening Task 1A — *Page 17*

Name of project _Monologue tape_   Due date _Next week_

Topic _Self-introduction_

Requirements _(1) Voice: clear, loud enough (2) Length: 5 to 10 minutes,_
(3) Don't read, speak freely from outline

Suggestions for preparation _Review grading criteria, complete the outline,_
record and grade, re-record and improve

Grading criteria _(1) Content: on topic? organized? interesting?_
(2) Presentation: loud and clear? enthusiastic? interesting?
pronunciation? grammar? (3) Mechanics: length? labeled? rewound?
on time?

EIKO: Hello, Mrs. Woods. I am Eiko Watanabe. I am from Japan, as you know. I would like to introduce myself and tell you why I am here in the United States and what I hope for my future. First, I will tell you about my family and where I am from. I am from Kyoto, Japan, a beautiful city famous for the royal palace. My father works for Mitsubishi, and my mother, my mother stays home with my two younger brothers, Hiro and Taka. They are both in elementary school. Hiro is in fourth grade and likes to get into trouble. He is not a bad boy; in fact he is quite charming and clever, and maybe that is why he is always getting into trouble. Taka is in sixth grade, and he is a very good student. I miss them a lot and call once a month and write every week. My mother has recently told me that my father may have a chance to work in the United States for a few years. She is not sure that it is a good time to leave Japan for Taka and Hiro, but I think they will learn English very quickly because they are so young. It might be hard for my mother, leaving Japan and moving here without knowing any English, but I could help her out. I get so excited when I think of the possibility of living with my family here in the United States, even if it is only for a few years.

About my reasons for coming to the United States, I am here as an F-1 visa student. I am taking mostly ESL classes now, but I want to major in Interior Design, because I love art and want to become a famous designer. I want to, I hope to transfer to a four-year college or university and get an art degree. I especially like a modern blend of East and West, so I think I could work either in Japan or in the United States. This semester I'm taking sixteen units: Art, PE, ESL Writing, and ESL Listening/Speaking. My favorite class is art, but I also like my listening/speaking class. I am in this class because listening and speaking are important, and I want to understand more of what people in the United States say. I want to learn not to be afraid to speak and to be more confident. I am afraid of speeches, but I know I have to give one in this class. I also want to understand Western culture, because I don't know whether I will live in the United States or Japan. Something very interesting about my life here is that I am in a homestay program and live with an American family, the Adams family. They have four people in their family. Mr. Adams works at a large bank, and Mrs. Adams works part time as a teacher. They have two daughters. Cindy is 16. She is a junior who goes out a lot and is very busy, but nice. She likes to play tennis and is learning to drive. Jennifer is 13 and is in seventh grade. She watches TV a lot and likes to rollerblade and swim, and she loves horses. Mr. and Mrs. Adams are very kind to me. They are so nice to have me stay with them, and they treat me very well. I hope they will come to visit me in Japan someday so I can show them my home and my city, Kyoto.

Now I will tell you about my daily schedule. Every day I take the bus to school, unless Mrs. Adams isn't working and can drop me off. I begin school at 8 A.M. and finish around 1p.m. I think it is very strange that there are classes at lunch time, but I have learned not to eat until 2 P.M., when I return home. I try to do my homework from 3 o'clock to 7 o'clock. The Adams usually eat dinner around 7 P.M., because Mr. Adams gets home late and the girls sometimes have activities after school. Sometimes we each have to eat whenever we can, because of all our different busy schedules. I like to watch TV with the family after dinner, because I can ask them about things I don't understand. On the weekends they rent movies, and I watch those, too. Jennifer likes to watch romantic comedies, and so do I. The family likes to go to the mountains or to the beach on three-day weekends. They have taken me skiing in the mountains nearby, and we have visited both San Diego and Santa Barbara. I don't think I am a very good skier, but I love to swim in the ocean. Santa Barbara is my favorite city in the United States so far. Maybe I can transfer to a school there: Then I can study at the beach every day! Well, thank you for listening to my tape, Mrs. Woods. I hope you enjoyed it. I got to introduce two families to you, the Watanabe family and the Adams family. See you in class.

THIEN: I am Thien Nguyen from Vietnam. I have a very interesting story about me, so I will tell you about an interesting trip I took in the United States when my friends and I drove to Las Vegas. We stayed for three nights in a hotel that was shaped like a triangle or pyramid, and we saw a fantastic show there. The food was not very good, but it was very cheap, and you could eat all you wanted. We had a great time playing the slot machines. I won $50, but then I lost it by playing more. If you have never seen Las Vegas at night with the thousands of lights, I suggest you go. Just watch out that you don't lose all your money gambling.

MARIA: Hello, Mrs. Woods. I am Maria Sanchez. I would like to introduce myself and tell you why I am here in the United States and what I hope for my future. First, I will tell you about my family and where I am from. I am from a beautiful coastal city near Guadalajara, Mexico, called Puerto Vallarta. I miss my beautiful city and relatives, but I visit every two years. I am married and have three children. Yes, the first is José. José is 2, Angela is 8, Antonio is 10, and I am 36. My husband works in a hardware and garden-supply store. We came to the United States to have more opportunities for our family. I want all my children to go to college. Even I am in college now. I am a good example for them. They see me doing my homework, and they say, "Mommy I want to go to college too, like you." Their English is better than mine. That's another reason why, umm, why I am here. Mrs. Woods, I must tell you, umm, because I am a mother of three children and now a student too, that I am a little worried about being too old to learn and about doing all the homework. Since I do all the work at home — the cleaning and cooking and everything — I do not have free time, except when two of my children are in school, and my youngest, José, naps. José stays at my brother's house when I'm at school, and I worry about that, too. Maybe I worry too much. I am taking two ESL classes, which is more than enough! After the children are all in school and my English is better, I hope to get a job so that all my kids can go to college. I want to buy a house, too, but that is in the future. Maybe someday I will be a teacher too. I want to be a bilingual teacher in elementary school because I love kids and I speak Spanish very well.

To become a teacher I have a long, long way to go, so I hope that this class will, ah, will help me improve my English. I need to speak more English and not be so shy. I want to pass this class and meet students from other countries. Thank you for listening to my tape, Mrs. Woods. I hope you were not bored. I did it over so many times I can't believe it. I will see you in class.

ABDUL: Hello, Mrs. Woods. I am Abdul Saeed. I would like to introduce myself and tell you why I am here in the United States and what I hope for my future. First, I will tell you about my family and where I am from. I am from Karachi, Pakistan. Pakistan is on the Arabian Sea and borders four countries: Iran and Afghanistan to the west, China to the north, and India to the east. Have you been to any of these countries? I have two older brothers, and they are both working in Karachi as doctors. My father owns a business there, and my mother stays at home to take care of him. I am the only one here, and I live with one of my uncles. I am here to get a degree. My father wants me to return to Pakistan and work with my brothers as a doctor, but I am not sure that is what I want, because I am interested in business. I live with my uncle and work full time at a mini-market, forty hours a week. I'm taking twelve units and want to transfer to a four-year university soon. I might want to study business law and live in the United States if I get a good job. In this class, I expect to have many opportunities to speak English. I want to prepare for classes at a university. I am a little worried about the number of projects in this class, but it should be no problem. I am interested in meeting people from different cultures. Thank you for your time. I hope you know me better now.

Answers for Listening Tasks 2A and 2C — *Page 18*

	Eiko	*Thien*	*Maria*	*Abdul*
1. Introduction	✔	✔	✔	✔
2. Family and country	✔		✔	✔
3. Reasons for coming	✔		✔	✔
4. Current situation	✔		✔	✔
5. Hopes and dreams	✔		✔	✔
6. Conclusion: This class			✔	✔

Answers for Listening Task 2D — *Page 18*

	Eiko	*Thien*	*Maria*	*Abdul*
Was the student's tape:				
on topic?	✔	___	✔	✔
well organized?	✔	___	✔	✔
interesting?	✔	___	✔	✔
loud and clear?	✔	✔	✔	✔
well practiced?	✔	___	✔	✔
enthusiastic?	✔	✔	✔	
spoken freely and not read?	✔	✔	✔	
OK in pronunciation?	✔	✔	✔	✔
OK in grammar?	✔	✔	✔	✔
5 to 10 minutes long?	✔	___	___	___
GRADE	A	D	B	C

Eiko's tape is well done and well organized. She covered almost all the points on the outline and followed the directions carefully.

Thien's tape is too short and is off topic. He did not follow the outline at all, and he ignored many of the directions. He did, however, turn it in on time and used a loud, clear voice.

Maria's tape is good; the music makes it interesting. She covered all the points on the outline and followed all the directions except that the tape was less than 5 minutes long.

Abdul's tape is a little too short, and he read from a paper instead of speaking freely from his outline.

▶ **CHAPTER 3**

Help with Vocabulary — *Page 26*

1. g, 2. b, 3. c, 4. a, 5. i, 6. j, 7. k, 8. h, 9. e, 10. f, 11. d

12. kind of (adv.)

13. from time to time (idiom)

14. As a matter of fact (idiom)

15. typical (adj.)

16. hold down a job (v., idiom)

17. survey (n.)

18. workload (n.)

19. pretty (adv.)

20. hectic (adj.)

21. cover the cost (v., idiom)

22. sponsor (v.)

Tapescript for Listening Task A — *Page 28*

UNCLE: Hello?

ABDUL: Hi, Uncle Muneeb. It's Abdul. I'm returning your call.

UNCLE: Abdul? Why aren't you at work? Is everything OK?

ABDUL: Everything is fine. I am at work. I'm on lunch break. It's the first chance I've had to call you back. Sorry it took me so long to get back to you.

UNCLE: No problem. I know how busy you are. In fact, that is why I had called you last week. How is everything going? Are you finding it too difficult working full time and taking twelve units of classes?

ABDUL: Well, it's not easy, but this is the way of life here. I'm sure most of my classmates are **holding down a job** or two and studying at the same time.

UNCLE: And how are your grades? Have you had any tests yet?

ABDUL: We just started, so we haven't had any tests. My ESL class is not hard, just a lot of work. **As a matter of fact,** I have to do a survey, and I was thinking of asking working students about their **workload.** Then I can prove to you that I am not the only one who is trying to study and work too.

UNCLE: Well, what about your other classes? You're taking a business class and a computer class too, aren't you?

ABDUL: Yeah. The computer class is not hard. I just need to find time to work on the projects at the computer lab. I'm **pretty** familiar with the terms and concepts because I have worked with computers before. The business class requires a lot of reading. I was trying to get through a chapter just now. The lectures are **kind of** boring, and I find it hard to take notes. I may ask someone if I can copy their notes to make sure I am getting everything.

UNCLE: That sounds like a good idea. You might try to get to know the professor too. Does he have office hours?

ABDUL: Yes. *She* does, but with my schedule, I'm lucky I can just get to class.

UNCLE: Is there anything I can do to help you?

ABDUL: Thanks, but right now I can't think of anything.

UNCLE: If things get too busy, remember your studies should come first. Did you need any money to **cover the cost** of the textbooks for the classes?

ABDUL: You know they *do* pay me **from time to time** for working here. Really, I'm fine. Thanks for all you have done; covering the tuition is more than enough.

UNCLE: OK. I'll let you eat your lunch and read that business chapter. Call if I can do anything for you.

ABDUL: I will. Talk to you later.

UNCLE: Bye.

ABDUL: Bye.

Answers for Post-Listening Task A — *Page 28*

1. b,   2. a,   3. a,   4. a,   5. c,   6. b,   7. c,   8. a

Tapescript for Post-Speaking Task 3A — *Page 37*

ABDUL: Hello. I'm Abdul and, ah, I was in this group over here. We decided to write our survey, on, on study habits of working students compared with non-working students. We defined a *working student* as someone who works more than 20 hours a week and takes at least twelve units of classes. OK, like all of you, the five of us in the group surveyed ten people each and, and so, we got 50 responses — 25 for working students and 25 for non-working students. I will report on question number 1. The question was, "How may hours do you study each week?" A. 0 to 5 hours, B. 6 to 10 hours, or C. 11 or more hours. We found that, well, you can see on this bar graph that the non-working students studied more hours each week. On the left, the numbers going up the left here, these are the number of people, like 0, 5, 10, 15, 20 people — who answered. The dark bars represent the working students, and the white ones are the non-working students. For the first answer, 10 working students said they studied between 0 and 5 hours each week, and only 3 non-working students studied that little. The second answer, which was 6 to 10 hours a week, was about even, with 11 working students and 9 non-working students. But you see here, the last, only *4* working students studied 11 or more hours a week, while *13* non-working students studied that much. Maybe it's easier to see the difference in the pie charts here. The first pie chart shows the study habits of the *working students*. A and B are the largest parts; 40 percent study 0 to 5 hours and 44 percent study 6 to 10 hours. Notice that only 16 percent study 11 or more hours a week. The next pie chart shows the study habits of the *non-working* students. C is the largest: 52 percent of non-working students study 11 or more hours a week. So our conclusion is that non-working students study more hours per week than working students do. Now Eiko will report on the second question.

► CHAPTER 4

Help with Vocabulary — *Page 58*

11	a. to not give up; to persevere, continue, carry on	hang in there (v.)
2	b. problem, worry	concern (n.)
1	c. sad, troubled, depressed	discouraged (adj.)
3	d. to cheer up, comfort, assure	encourage (v.)
7	e. used to introduce evidence or proof	just by the fact that (idiom)
10	f. to use to one's own benefit	take advantage of (v.)
5	g. to sense or have a feeling of belonging	fit in (v.)

8	h. to act in a way that shows something is important	take seriously (v.)
12	i. fair, right, sensible, rational	reasonable (adj.)
9	j. devoted to	dedicated (adj.)
4	k. the ability to endure, to accept but not share	tolerance (n.)
6	l. a movie that makes you want to cry	tearjerker (n.)

Answers for Listening Task 2A — *Pages 60–61*

1.	tired	13.	encouraged
2.	really	14.	**dedicated**
3.	bothering	15.	am **taking** it too **seriously**
4.	truth	16.	**reasonable**
5.	discouraged	17.	**hang in there**
6.	concerns	18.	**take advantage of**
7.	worried	19.	**tearjerker**
8.	pretty	20.	fiction
9.	**fit in**	21.	romantic
10.	kids	22.	feeling
11.	matter	23.	choose
12.	**Just by the fact that**	24.	same

Answers for Pre-Speaking Task 1C — *Page 63*

G = General audiences
PG = Parental guidance suggested
PG13 = Parental guidance for those age 13 and under
R = Restricted for those over 18 unless accompanied
by a parent or guardian
X = Adults only

Tapescript for Speaking Task A — *Page 69*

MARIA: I watched the movie *Stand and Deliver* and I really liked it. Five stars! Two thumbs up! It's an old movie — well, not that old, 1988 — and it is rated PG. The setting is, umm, the 1980s, and it's at a high school in the inner city, East Los Angeles. The school is really dangerous and wild because of gangs, and well, it's, it's in a bad part of town. The major character is the teacher Jamie Escalante. He can speak Spanish. He is this really nice guy who quits a good job just to be a teacher to help the students. He thinks he can help change them, to help them believe in themselves. Well, he has to teach this summer school class of a bunch of losers. These kids don't want to learn, and they give him a hard time. He is real creative though, and he, he gets their attention, by, ah, well once he comes dressed as a chef and brings a knife and cuts an apple in parts to teach fractions.

He makes math easy to understand. So the kids begin to like him, and they learn math and even advanced-placement calculus. They take this really hard exam and pass, but the testing committee thinks they must have cheated because they think the kids are too stupid to, to be able to pass. It's kind of like discrimination because most of the kids are minorities and have Spanish last names. Anyway, the students retake the test and pass it again. I cried, it was so great. The teacher teaches them to not give up even, umm, under discrimination. It made me want to be a teacher and make a difference, too. I really recommend this movie. /

▶ CHAPTER 5

Help with Vocabulary — *Page 72*

6	a.	to make someone who is sad feel better	cheer up (v.)
9	b.	upright, straight up and down	vertical (adj.)
1	c.	to have a good time in honor of an achievement	celebrate (v.)
14	d.	to bargain	negotiate (v.)
13	e.	from left to right or side to side	horizontal (adj.)
7	f.	firmness or thickness of a liquid	consistency (n.)
5	g.	to serve yourself	help myself (v.)
12	h.	terrible, sad, unfortunate	tragic (adj.)
10	i.	a line on which things are drawn symmetrically	axis (n.)
4	j.	prepared food that has not been consumed and is saved	leftovers (n.)
2	k.	University of California at Los Angeles	UCLA (n.)
3	l.	a program that houses foreign students with native families	homestay (adj.)
11	m.	to take in	adopt (v.)
8	n.	a comparison of two things in order to explain a point	analogy (n.)

Tapescript for Listening Tasks 1A and 1B — *Pages 73–74*

EIKO: Today is Friday, and it's my little brother's birthday. I tried to call home, but nobody answered. They must have gone out to **celebrate.** I hope he got the card and gift I sent. He'll love the **UCLA** shirt I got him. I wish I could be there now to see what they are doing, but I know that it is important to be here and learn English. At times I wish I could be in two places at once.

Things at school are going well. I got an *A* on my movie review, my monologue tape, and my survey. The first three speaking projects were a lot of work, but I had fun doing them. The next project is an interview. Since I have to interview one English speaker born in the United States, I was thinking of interviewing Cindy, my **homestay** "sister." Actually, we are not like sisters at all, because we are so different. Maybe I can ask her about the some aspects of this country's culture that I don't understand.

The hardest thing about living here, besides missing my family, is meal time. Sometimes my homestay family skips meals, or they all eat dinner on their own. Everyone gets something from the refrigerator and eats at different times in different places. Cindy likes to eat in her room while talking on the phone. There are a lot of boys who call. Jennifer, who is 13, likes to eat in front of the TV. I feel strange getting my own meal, even though they showed me how to warm up **leftovers** and frozen food in the microwave. It's hard for me to **"help myself"** when it is not my own house. I miss helping my mother prepare Japanese food and eating with my family. Last week we went out to a Japanese restaurant. It was very good, and they let me order for the whole family. The girls didn't eat much, but they tried a bite of everything. Now they know how I feel eating strange foods.

Sometimes when I cannot understand the jokes on TV and I am tired of making my tongue speak English, I close the door to my room and write to my friends or write in this journal. Mrs. Adams worries that I am sad, but I need to be alone sometimes, that is all. Sometimes I cry because I miss my friends so much, but something always happens to **cheer** me **up.** When I get a letter from Japan, that makes me happy for two days. My mother says that I am forgetting my Japanese. If I forget my Japanese before I learn English, what language will I speak?

Answers for Listening Task 1B — *Page 74*

1. F,   2. T,   3. T,   4. F,   5. F,   6. T,   7. F,   8. T,   9. T,   10. F,   11. T,   12. F

Tapescript and Answers for Listening Tasks 2A through 2C — *Page 77*

NON-NATIVE SPEAKER: Do you ever tell to a friend to "borrow you" some money?*

NATIVE SPEAKER: Borrow you some money? **(2)** Do you mean "lend you" some money? **(1)** Do I ever ask my friends *to lend* me money? **(1)**

NON-NATIVE SPEAKER: Yes. *Lend you* money; that's what I mean. **(4)**

NATIVE SPEAKER: Well, it all depends on, you know, how well I know them, and all. Like, if they owe me any favors and stuff like that. I mean I would, I guess, if I really needed it and it wasn't that much, say $20 or $40. But I wouldn't go around borrowing $200 from friends. Besides, who has that much cash to give away? When I need....

NON-NATIVE SPEAKER: Excuse me. I'm confused a bit. Is your answer yes or no? **(1)** I have to write down yes or no.

NATIVE SPEAKER: Let's say yes. That is, if it's under 50 bucks, a good friend, and I really need it.

NON-NATIVE SPEAKER: Could you repeat that last part a bit slower, please? **(3)** and **(5)**

NATIVE SPEAKER: I'm sorry. I speak fast, don't I? I borrow money if it is under $50, if I'm borrowing from a good friend, and if I really need the money. Just write yes.

► VOCABULARY REVIEW

Answers for Chapters 1 to 5 — *Pages 87–96*

Chapter 1: *Mean Mr. Miller, the Math Teacher*

1. down for a nap, 2. anxious, 3. strict, 4. probation, 5. shift,
6. jot down, 7. chicken out, 8. embarrassed, 9. demanding, 10. GPA,
11. keep track of, 12. frustrate, 13. suicide, 14. entrepreneur

Chapter 2: *Are You Willing to Wait?*

1. advantage, 2. end up, 3. enthusiastic, 4. interrupt, 5. feedback,
6. challenge, 7. glance, 8. disadvantage, 9. clarification, 10. hinder,
11. strategy

Chapter 3: *Covering the Cost of College*

1. pretty (*or* kind of), 2. kind of (*or* pretty), 3. cover the cost,
4. As a matter of fact, 5. hectic, 6. hold down, 7. workload, 8. sponsor,
9. survey, 10. typical, 11. from time to time

Chapter 4: *Careers Are Us*

1. discouraged, 2. tearjerker, 3. hang in there, 4. fit in, 5. take advantage of,
6. take seriously, 7. concern, 8. dedicated, 9. encouraging,
10. reasonable, 11. Just by the fact that, 12. tolerate

Chapter 5: *Leftover "Soup"*

1. tragic, 2. UCLA, 3. homestay, 4. cheer her up, 5. adopt,
6. help herself, 7. negotiate, 8. celebrate, 9. vertical, 10. axis,
11. horizontal, 12. axis, 13. consistency, 14. leftover

CHAPTER 6

Help with Vocabulary — *Page 98*

1. i, 2. k, 3. h, 4. c, 5. a, 6. d, 7. b, 8. l, 9. j, 10. f, 11. g, 12. e
13. enormous (adj.)
14. slip (v.)
15. impromptu (adj.)
16. adjacent (adj.)
17. motivation (n.)
18. or else (idiom)
19. lottery (n.)
20. fondest (adj.)
21. cannot stand (v.)
22. stand out (v.)
23. stressed out (v.)
24. confident (adj.)

Tapescript for Listening Tasks A and C — *Page 100*

MRS. WOODS: Hi, Thien. I'm glad you came to see me. Come on in, and have a seat. Let me move these papers out of your way. Here you go.

THIEN: Thank you.

MRS. WOODS: What can I do for you, Thein?

THIEN: After I looked over my grades last week, I was concerned about my lack of progress, and that's why I came to see you, Mrs. Woods.

MRS. WOODS: Let's have a look at your grades. It seems that you have a *D* average. Your tape project was a low *D* because it was off topic and you did not follow the directions. The survey was late and incomplete, so you got an *F* on that. I see your movie review was well done, a *B*, so I know you can do the work when you apply yourself; but the interview was late and not done according to the directions, so that was a *D*. What do you think the problem is?

THIEN: I didn't like the survey and the interview. I **cannot stand** to speak English to people I don't know. Before I came to this country, I had a lot of friends, and we had a lot of good times. Now, all I do is study. Sometimes I just want to go home, but I know I can't. If I could only speak better, I ... I don't know.

MRS. WOODS: That's an honest answer and an understandable one, too, but that is all the more reason that you should continue with this class so you can get more comfortable speaking with others. Hmm. Let's not worry about the three poor grades so far; they are in the past. But concentrate on the future projects, and see what you can do to pull your grades up — that is, if you still want to hang in there and work hard to raise your grades. What do you think?

THIEN: I have to stay in this class and get above a 2-point average because I'm on probation. I need to have twelve units and to bring my GPA up this semester or I'll have to drop out completely for a year.

MRS. WOODS: I was hoping the **motivation** would come from inside yourself. I mean, if you want to do well because you want to succeed, you'll do much better than if someone else is telling you have to do this **or else!** Do you want to improve your spoken English?

THIEN: Yes. Of course.

MRS. WOODS: Well think of that to motivate you. You are doing these projects to help you speak better English, which is your goal. Let me help you prepare for the next project, the impromptu speech. Make an appointment to come to my office again, and we'll practice a few times so it will be easier for you in class. How does that sound?

THIEN: That sounds good.

MRS. WOODS: Great. I think you can do it.

THIEN: Yeah. I think I can, too. It's almost time for class. I'll see you in the classroom.

MRS. WOODS: Bye, Thien. And don't forget to come see me before the end of next week for the practice impromptu speech.

THIEN: I won't forget. Bye.

Answers for Listening Tasks A and C — *Page 100*

A. 1. concerned, understanding, encouraging, helpful
   2. shy, honest, embarrassed
C. 3 Thien's low grades; his lack of progress
   4. Thien didn't like the survey and the interview because he doesn't like speaking to strangers.
   5. Thien wants to stay above a 2-point average and keep twelve units of classes because he's on probation.
   6. She wanted to help Thien prepare for the next project.

Tapescript for Pre-Speaking Tasks 2B and 2C — *Page 102*

THIEN: Have you ever lost a friend to a bullet? I have. That is why I think there should be stricter gun control laws in the United States. It happened just last year. It was New Year's Eve, and everyone was celebrating, setting off firecrackers, and drinking to bring the new year in with a "bang." When it struck midnight, a guy with a handgun fired some rounds into the air, and seconds later my friend lay dead beside me, hit by a stray bullet. He died before they even put him in the ambulance.

What do you think about gun control? I support stricter gun control laws for three reasons. First, if guns had not been so easy to buy, so easy to own, and so easy to have in public, my friend might be alive today. Second, with stricter laws, many other innocent victims would also be alive today as well. If you own a gun, you and those who live with you are many more times likely to die from a gunshot wound than someone who doesn't own a gun. Those are the facts. Finally, stricter gun control laws are needed because in the major cities in the United States the number-1 killer among young people like ourselves is gunshot wounds. My three reasons for stricter laws are personal. They are my dead friend, other innocent victims like him, and finally you and me. Those are pretty important reasons. Now, how should you vote on gun control laws? The answer is easy. Thank you.

Answers for Pre-Speaking Task 2C — *Page 102*

Note's from Thien's Impromptu Speech

Attention-grabbing comment or question   Have you ever lost a friend to a bullet?

Clearly stated main idea   There should be stricter gun control laws in the United States.

Body of speech

1. First, if guns had not been so easy to buy, my friend might be alive.

2. Second, with stricter laws, many other innocent victims would be alive.

3. The number-1 killer among young people is gunshot wounds.

Conclusion   My three reasons for stricter laws are personal. They are my dead friend, other innocent victims like him, and finally you and me.

CHAPTER 7

Help with Vocabulary — *Page 108*

5	a.	something proposed, a subject to be discussed	proposition (n.)
9	b.	a short, entertaining story	anecdote (n.)
1	c.	to be amazed, in wonder with fear and respect	stand in awe (v.)
2	d.	debatable, having opposing sides	controversial (adj.)
7	e.	a close relationship, agreement, harmony	rapport (n.)
8	f.	to give, to set aside for	allot (v.)
6	g.	having to do with, relating to	relevant (adj.)
3	h.	to convince, to talk into	persuade (v.)
10	i.	to prove to be wrong	refute (v.)
11	j.	not correct	inaccurate (adj.)
12	k.	prejudiced, in favor or against someone	biased (adj.)
4	l.	a hindrance, something that prevents or stops something else	deterrent (n.)

Answers for Pre-Listening Tasks B and C — *Pages 109–110*

B. Prepare and deliver an effective speech.
C. 1. Determine the purpose.
2. Assess the audience.
3. Select and narrow the topic.
4. Gather material.
5. Organize an outline.
6. Deliver the speech based on the outline.

Tapescript for Listening Task 1A and 2A — *Pages 110–113*

MRS. WOODS: In just one or two weeks, you will be standing up here in front of the class ready to deliver your 10-minute speech. You'll glance at your outline and then look confidently into the eyes of the people in your audience and present your points in an organized and convincing manner. You'll have a visual aid, such as a poster with a graph illustrating statistics that support one of your points. Maybe you'll have a handout like the one I provided of the outline of this speech. And before you know it, the speech will be over. Your classmates will applaud and **stand in awe** of your speech as you take your seat. Is this just a dream? Maybe not. My objective today is to enable you to prepare and deliver an effective 10-minute speech. As you can see on the outline provided, there are six steps. The first one is "Determine the purpose of the speech." Traditionally, speeches have three purposes: to **persuade,** to inform, and to entertain. The topic of a persuasive speech is always **controversial**, such as gun control, abortion, or the death penalty. The speaker of a persuasive speech tries to persuade the audience to believe his or her **proposition.** For example, if one's proposition is that the death penalty is a **deterrent** to crime and should be used more often, a speaker would try to convince the audience with case studies, statistics, and other evidence. An informative speech informs or instructs. The topic of an informative speech might be, umm, how to lose weight and keep it off, for example. An entertaining speech entertains, like the speech a football player might give at a dinner to celebrate the team's championship. You will choose one of the first two purposes; persuasive and informative speeches are common in academic and business settings.

OK, well, after you determine the purpose of your speech, step 2 is "Assess your audience." That means finding out *who* your audience is. You will see that this is very important to know before you select a specific topic. Who will be *your* audience for this speech? Yes, your classmates. Just look around you. Why is it important to know your audience? As you can see from item A1 under step 2 on the outline, knowing the audience helps you choose a **relevant** topic, or one that the audience can relate to. Well, let's say you wanted to give a speech about, about, how to, to invest your money in the stock market, and most of your suggestions required investors to have thousands of dollars. If your audience consisted of people who did not have thousands of dollars to invest, or of people who did not trust or understand this type of investment, the speech would not be successful. Knowing the audience also helps in building **rapport.** *Rapport* refers to the relationship between the speaker and the audience, the interaction, the, the communication. Rapport can be measured by the expressions on the faces of the audience. Are they wide-eyed and following the speech, or, like Paul there in the back — "Hi, Paul! Are you awake? Just checking"—are they falling asleep? See, if you know your audience, you can build rapport because you know what topic to choose, what examples to use, what objections the audience might have to your points, and so on; and this leads into my third point, which is persuasion. Knowing the needs, wants, and background of your audience gives you the power to persuade them to come around to your point of view. Now, when I say you should know who your audience is, the factors to consider are under step 2, point B: the education level and the general world knowledge of your audience, their profession or specialty knowledge, and personal information, such as age, gender, what country they come from, where they live, how much money they make, and so on.

Now, step 3 is "Select and narrow the topic." You already know that the topic must be appropriate and relevant to your specific audience, but where do you begin apart from that? Basically, you have two choices. The first is, ah, a topic you know a lot about—and if you don't have a lot of time, that's the way to go. The other choice is to select a topic you wish you knew about. It's a good idea to think about classes you have taken, or, or shows you've seen. What magazines do you like to read? Or maybe your hobbies and talents you have are the basis of a topic. What do you do with your leisure time? What trips have you taken? What news items do you read about? So, once you choose a topic, you need to narrow it down. Your speech can only be 10 minutes, and that is not a lot of time.

So if you want to say something significant about your topic — something your audience doesn't already know — you will want to narrow it down to fit in the time **allotted.** You want to go deep into a narrow topic rather than just touching the surface of a broader, general topic. To narrow down your topic, think about your objective, or what you want your audience to be able to *know* or *do* after your speech is over. The objective of *this* speech is to enable you to prepare and deliver an effective 10-minute speech. So think about what you want the audience to be able to do after your speech; that should produce an objective for you.

Step 4 is "Gather material." Most likely, you will go to the library. You could find books. Books are good — but long and sometimes old. A better source will probably be magazines or periodicals. You can use the *Reader's Guide to Periodicals* to find the right articles. Other sources are the media, such as TV documentaries or interviews with people who know a lot about your topic. You could even use some past personal experiences or lectures you have heard. All this is useful information that you can use in your speech. Then, after you have gathered the material from the library and these other sources, you need to organize it into an outline, which is step 5.

Everyone must have an outline and turn it in before the date of the speech. I want you to follow formal outline format, and I've given you an example right there in your hand. Notice that all my major points — and I have six of them, because I have six steps, are closest to the left-hand margin of the paper and are set off by capital Roman numerals made up of *I*s and *V*s. You see that? Now, I've indented from there, and I have capital letters for the next level of support, capital *A, B, C,* and *D.* When I break it down further, I have indented even more, and now I use what? *1, 2, 3,* right — Arabic numerals. And if I wanted to break it down one more level, what would I use? Lower-case letters: small *a*, small *b*, and so on. But in my outline I haven't gone that far, have I?

When you actually begin your speech, however, the first words out of your mouth won't be your first point. You will first need to grab the attention of the audience. Wake them up. Make them pay attention to you! How do you do this? You use an attention-grabbing device. One way is to ask a question like, Do you know what the major cause of death is for young people like ourselves? Another way is to use a thought-provoking statement. I did that by stating that you would be standing in front of the class in a week or two. Quoting someone, which means using his or her exact words and noting who said them, is effective if the quote relates to your topic. A short funny story, or **anecdote,** is also attention-grabbing, but remember that it must be short, because you only have 10 minutes. There are only two comments I will make about the body of the speech. First is that it should be logically developed, which means that the flow of thought is logical and understandable. Second, the points must be adequately supported, which means that you must have enough examples, proof, or evidence. In a persuasive speech — which, as you know, must be about a controversial topic — you should **refute** the counterarguments as well, showing that they are invalid or **inaccurate,** but do it in a respectful way that is free of **bias** so that your audience can see that you have treated the opposing side fairly. Finally, end with a conclusion, which restates the major points and brings closure to the speech.

The sixth and last step is "Deliver the speech based on the outline." You must practice, practice, practice! A good way to practice at home is to go into your bathroom, shut and lock the door, check your watch, glance at your outline, look into the mirror, and deliver your speech. When you have finished, check your watch again to see how long the speech was. That's how you practice. Another way is to put the speech on tape. Record yourself. Listen to yourself, and tape it again to improve it. Better yet, give your speech live to a critical audience, such as your family or friends. Ask them how to improve the speech. They'll probably tell you. You are also required to have a visual aid. By that I mean anything relating to your speech that the audience can see. You can use a handout, a poster, or a flip chart. The content could be your outline, a map, a chart, or photographs. You may use the chalkboard briefly, but you must use another visual aid besides that. And be sure not to turn your back to your audience when using the chalkboard. Whatever visual aid you use, make sure it has a specific purpose in your speech, such as to clarify a complex point or to illustrate a major point dramatically.

I'm almost done — just two more points. Let me speak briefly about language and then appearance. Regarding language, and more specifically pronunciation, if you know you have problems with certain words you plan to use, bring a tape to class, and I'll record them for you to practice. When you use that word in your speech, you could write it on the chalkboard and point to it later in the speech when you use it again. The most important point about language is that you must speak naturally, as though you were having a conversation. *Do not* read your speech, and never try to memorize it. That makes the audience as nervous as the speaker. Your appearance should be neat but not overdone. The message is only as reliable as the messenger. You want your audience to think about your message, not about you. You need good posture. Try to stand relaxed and show confidence at the podium, using your hands to illustrate your points and using your eyes to keep in touch with your audience. Maintain good eye contact.

In conclusion then, if you follow these six steps, I think you will be able to prepare for and deliver an effective 10-minute speech. Thank you.

Answers for Listening Tasks 2A through 2F — *Pages 110–113*

A. 1. In just one or two weeks, you will be standing up here in front of the class ready to deliver your 10-minute speech.

2. Pay attention, because we have to give a speech soon.

3. To enable us to prepare and deliver an effective 10-minute speech.

4. To **persuade** the audience to act or believe in a certain way.

5. The topic of a persuasive speech is always **controversial.**

B. 6. To find out who our audience is.

7. It helps us choose a **relevant** topic, helps in building **rapport,** and helps us know how to persuade the audience.

8. Rapport is the relationship the speaker has with the audience; it can be measured by the facial expressions of audience members.

9. Rapport influences the topic, the examples, and how to present the speech.

C. 10. Choose a topic we know a lot about or one we *wish* we knew about.

11. Classes we have taken, shows we have seen, magazines we like to read, our hobbies and talents, our leisure-time activities, trips we have taken, news items we read.

12. The speech can only be 10 minutes, so we need to narrow the topic down to fit in the time allotted. We should go deep into a narrow topic rather than just touching the surface of a broader, general topic.

13. What do I want the audience to know or be able to do after my speech?

D. 14. Periodicals are shorter and more up to date than books.

15. The media, such as TV documentaries or interviews with people who know a lot about my topic or even some past personal experiences or lectures.

E. 16. Roman numerals.

17. A question, a thought-provoking statement, a quote, an anecdote, or a startling statistic.

18. The flow of thought is logical and understandable.

19. There must be enough examples, proof, or evidence.

20. Refute the counterarguments in a respectful way that is free of bias.

F. 21. Practice in private at home; record myself; practice in front of family or friends.

22. Answers will vary.

23. A handout, a poster, or a flip chart.

24. A map, the outline, a chart, or photographs.

25. To clarify a complex point or illustrate a major point dramatically.

26. Before the speech have the instructor or some native speaker record the words on tape so I can practice; during the speech write the word on the chalkboard and point to it when using it.

27. A memorized speech can make the audience as nervous as the speaker.

28. If the messenger cannot be believed or taken seriously, the message will not be believed or taken seriously.

29. I should stand relaxed with confidence.

30. Use our hands to illustrate points; maintain good eye contact.

Answers for Post-Listening Tasks A and C — *Page 116*

Note: Answers will vary, but there should be a logical reason for the order.

A.

I. Males
   A. Fathers
   B. Uncles
      1. Uncle Bruce
      2. Uncle Sam
      3. Uncle Dick
   C. Husbands
   D. Brothers
      1. Brother Bill
      2. Brother John

II. Females
   A. Mothers
   B. Aunts
      1. Aunt Cindy
      2. Aunt Louise
      3. Aunt Ann
   C. Wives
   D. Sisters
      1. Sister Laura
      2. Sister Karen

C.

1. Speech about a Disease
   I. Introduction
      A. Definition
      B. Brief background
   II. Symptoms
   III. Causes
   IV. Treatment
   V. Prevention
   VI. Conclusion

2. Speech about a Controversial Topic
   I. Introduction
      A. Definition
      B. Brief background
   II. Arguments in favor
   III. Arguments against
   IV. Conclusion

3. Speech about How to Do Something
   I. Introduction
      A. Definition
      B. Brief background
   II. Why it is beneficial
   III. How to do it
   IV. Conclusion

4. Speech about a Social Problem

    I.   Introduction

        A. Definition

        B. Brief background

   II.   Cause

 III. Effects

 IV. Prevention

   V. Conclusion

▶ **CHAPTER 8**

Help with Vocabulary — *Page 130*

4	a. to give up something of value in order to achieve something else	sacrifice (v.)
2	b. in contest against	versus (prep.)
9	c. to destroy, do away with, end completely	abolish (v.)
10	d. the act or method of causing death painlessly	euthanasia (n.)
12	e. a person who is being held in jail or an institution	inmate (n.)
6	f. the side of a team that must score points or attack	offensive (adj.)
8	g. to give jointly with a group of others	contribute (v.)
11	h. a means of examining things to remove objectionable content	censorship (n.)
7	i. the side of a team that defends the goal or position	defensive (adj.)
5	j. to question closely to find out the truth	cross-examine (v.)
13	k. required, something that must be done	mandatory (adj.)
1	l. to plan, make, build	construct (v.)
3	m. in humans, the unborn young from the end of the third month to birth	fetus (n.)

Tapescript for Listening Tasks A and C — *Pages 132–133*

MONITOR: Welcome to our debate today about a change in policy regarding abortion. As you see on the board, the proposition to be debated is "Abortion should be made illegal in the USA." Representing the affirmative side — those in favor of changing the current law to make abortions illegal — are Maria, Rosa, Paul, and Anton. Representing the negative side — those against any change in the current law that permits abortion — are Thien, Marcelo, Nelly, and Tru. We will now begin our debate with the affirmative side. You have 6 minutes to **construct** your case.

MARIA: Thank you. We believe that abortion should once again be made illegal in the United States because we consider it to be the taking of a human life. Worst of all, it involves the decision to terminate a pregnancy. Who can argue that abortion is not ending a life? What is in the woman's womb is alive, isn't it? Therefore, abortion is the taking of a human life. Those who favor abortion call themselves "pro-choice." They believe women should have the right to have a choice of whether to have their baby or not. But the choice they are making is, in fact, the end of the life of a fetus. The U.S. Supreme Court's ruling on Roe **versus** Wade in 1973 legalized abortion on demand in the early stages of pregnancy and gave states the right to protect the rights of the **fetus** in later stages of pregnancy, when the fetus was capable of living outside the womb, or at twenty-four weeks. Did they ever imagine that today there would be 1.5 million abortions a year, or 4,000 abortions each day? Did they ever imagine that some women may have regrets later on after having an abortion? Did they ever imagine that some women would choose to have abortions because the child they were carrying in their womb was not the desired sex or was not conceived at a convenient time for their careers? We believe that abortion is wrong. It is a bad solution to a complex problem. There are better solutions to this problem, which my teammate Rosa will discuss. Rosa.

ROSA: Thank you, Maria. A teenage girl, let's call her Lisa, is faced with an unwanted pregnancy. What are her options? Today she could choose abortion up to the twenty-fourth week. That's into the sixth month. After being told that she is carrying a boy and hearing the heartbeat, Lisa wonders if abortion is justified just because she doesn't want him. If she chose to have her son, what would happen? In most cases the unwanted child becomes wanted after birth. The mother sees her own son or daughter in need of love and care and bonds with the baby. She is ready to **sacrifice** whatever it may take to raise the child. But if Lisa does not have a change of heart or is unable to care for the child, she could give her son to a couple who is able to care for him, and thus provide a loving, caring environment for him through adoption. This also solves the couple's problem of desperately wanting a child, but being unable to have one. By making abortion illegal, we are still giving Lisa a choice. She can choose to keep her son or give him up for adoption, but the choice to abort the fetus would not be an option. Lisa is at one of the most emotional times of her life. She is confused and unaware of the negative impact the wrong choice could have on her later in life. Abortion sounds like a quick fix to a messy problem to her. We believe it is the wrong choice. So once again we state that abortion should be made illegal because it is the taking of a human life and, second, there are better options, such as keeping the child or giving the child up for adoption. Thank you.

MONITOR: Thank you, Maria and Rosa. Now it is time for the opposing side to **cross-examine.** You have 3 minutes.

NELLY: I think that we need to ask the question that the abortion debate is based on. And that is, when does human life begin? Clearly, Rosa and Maria believe that it begins at conception, when the sperm meets the egg. Therefore, they feel that ending the pregnancy after that moment, is in fact the taking of a human life. They feel that the just-fertilized egg is a full human being and should be protected. But it should be made clear that there is no agreement or consensus to this question of when human life begins. Many people believe that human life begins at about twenty weeks of pregnancy, when the fetus can live on its own, when it is viable. The government seems to agree, for it allows states to prohibit abortions after twenty weeks or after viability. Since there is no consensus on when human life begins, and there is little hope for compromise, don't you think that it should be up to the woman to decide to terminate her own pregnancy? A significant majority of people in the United States agree that a woman should have free access to abortion in the first trimester of pregnancy.

ROSA: Nelly, I think you are right about the basic question we need to answer, which is, when does human life begin? Since we believe that human life begins at conception, we see abortion at any stage as the taking of a human life and so it should be punishable by law. In answer to your question, it is our opinion that the woman should not be permitted to end her pregnancy.

TRU: I agree with Nelly. You seem to think that some women feel regret after an abortion. I read, however, that the most common feeling after an abortion is relief. Sometimes it is in the best interest of the woman and the fetus to end the pregnancy. What about the cases of medical complications, such as fetal abnormalities, tragic events like rape or incest, teenage pregnancy, or the lack of money?

PAUL: We think that abortion is wrong, and so it should be illegal, but there may be cases when it is permitted such as when the life of the mother is at risk and so the life of the unborn child must be sacrificed.

THIEN: I want to ask about the conditions of women before abortion became legal. We know that many women found ways to get abortions even though they were illegal, and many died or suffered at the hands of those attempting abortions in unclean conditions. Do you want to go back to those times? Most people want abortions to be safe, and the only way to make them safe is to make them legal.

ANTON: I'll answer that. Thien, it is safer for a woman to get an abortion now than it was back when abortions were illegal. But if we consider the fetus a life, there have been more fetal deaths caused by abortions than women dying due to complications during abortions.

MONITOR: Thank you. I'm sorry, but the cross-examination is over, and the audience now has 3 minutes to ask the affirmative side questions.

CLASSMATE 1: Don't' you think that if abortions were made illegal that there would be a rise in child abuse?

ROSA: If you consider abortion the termination of life, then abortion itself could be considered a form of child abuse. Although there is much debate on the issue, some feel that the fetus feels pain when aborted.

CLASSMATE 2: Rosa, you just said that the fetus can feel pain, but that has not been proven. Besides, in most cases, it is not a fetus we are discussing, it is a newly fertilized egg. The National Abortion Federation states that 90 percent of the abortions in the United States are done in the first trimester and less than 1 percent after twenty-one weeks. Over half of all abortions are performed in the first eight weeks. At that point what is in the woman's womb is not even called a fetus.

MARIA: That newly fertilized egg, as you said, is alive and it is human, so it is a human being.

CLASSMATE 2: In that case, what about the hundreds of eggs that a woman releases in a lifetime, or for that matter, the millions of sperms a man ejects. They, too, are alive and are human, but no one calls them human life, or grieves at their loss. The human being that is being sacrificed is not the fetus but the woman who is being stripped of her rights.

CLASSMATE 3: Yes, I agree. The woman is the human being in this picture, not the fetus. Having a baby drastically changes a woman's life. Women should have the right to choose what to do with their bodies, not the government. My sister's friend got an abortion because she wanted to graduate from college. She also had a job lined up after graduation. She would have lost that job if she had had that baby. Not only that, she wasn't ready for the responsibility of raising a child alone. She would have had to go on welfare and then she would have blamed the baby for messing up her life. I think the government should mind its own business and let the woman whose life will be drastically changed make the choice, don't you?

PAUL: Your sister's friend and her partner knew the possible consequences of their actions. She and the father of the baby should have taken the responsibility for the pregnancy which resulted, however inconvenient this may have made their lives. They should have kept the baby or given it up for adoption.

CLASSMATE 4: Paul, you can't make that decision for her. Only the pregnant woman can decide whether she wants to have an abortion or not. You should not have the right to tell others who don't believe that the fetus is a human life that they have to have a baby if they don't want to. It seems...

MONITOR: Thank you. Time is up. It is now time for the negative side to construct it's case.

Answers for Listening Task A — *Pages 132–133*

Maria's main point: Abortion is the taking of a human life.

Rosa's main point: There are better options, such as keeping the child or giving the child up for adoption.

Issues raised : When does human life begin, the consequences of illegal abortions, unwanted children, abortions for victims of rape and incest, child abuse, the rights of women.

▶ CHAPTER 9

Help with Vocabulary — *Page 144*

1. l, 2. c, 3. i, 4. h, 5. a, 6. d, 7. k, 8. e, 9. f, 10. j, 11. b, 12. g

13. eliminate (v.)

14. lift (n.)

15. keep on the lookout for (v., idiom)

16. inadequacy (n.)

17. attain (v.)

18. samosa (n.)

19. potluck (adj.)

20. put off (v.)

21. brainstorm (v.)

22. prop (n.)

23. résumé (n.)

24. mentioned (v.)

Tapescript for Listening Tasks 1A and 1B — *Pages 146–147*

THIEN: Abdul, thank you for making me come to this party. I have met some new people, and I have been speaking English the whole time.

ABDUL: And you thought you wouldn't like it. I told you the International Students' Club is really fun. Besides, the food is always interesting at these potluck parties. Did you try the **samosa?** I love that stuff.

THIEN: The what? I don't think so. Hey! Isn't that Eiko over there?

ABDUL: Yeah. Let's go see her.

EIKO:	Well, look who's here. Abdul and Thien. Thien, I didn't know you were interested in the ISC. When did you start coming?
THIEN:	ISC? Oh, the International Students' Club. Well I just came today because Abdul made me, but I have to admit I kind of like it.
EIKO:	Good. Then that means you will want to become a member. I have been looking for some help making the posters to advertise the club meetings. You're good at art. How about helping me out once in a while?
THIEN:	Well, yeah. I don't see why not.
EIKO:	Oh, I'm sorry; I didn't introduce you to my friend. Kyung Hee, this is Thien and Abdul, two guys in my ESL class. Thien and Abdul, this is Kyung Hee. She's from Korea.
ABDUL:	Hi. It's nice to meet you.
KYUNG HEE:	Nice to meet you, too.
THIEN:	Haven't I seen you in another class before? Did you take writing last semester with Mr. Winters?
KYUNG HEE:	Yes, but I don't remember you from that class.
THIEN:	Maybe that's because I dropped out after a few weeks. Too many papers!
KYUNG HEE:	That's for sure. I have never written so much in my life.
ABDUL:	Speaking of writing, that reminds me. I've been here for over an hour, and I have a business paper that I need to work on. Thien, do you want to come with me, or can you catch a ride back with someone else?
EIKO:	Mrs. Adams can give you a **lift** home, Thien, if you want to stay. She is picking me up at 5 o'clock and she won't mind, I'm sure.
THIEN:	Well, if you're sure she won't mind.
ABDUL:	Great! I guess I'll see you all at school. Bye. And nice meeting you, Kyung Hee.
EIKO:	Bye, Abdul.
KYUNG HEE:	Bye.
THIEN:	See you, and thanks again.

Answers for Listening Task 1B — *Pages 146–147*

1. b,   2. c,   3. a,   4. b,   5. c,   6. b,   7. c,   8. c

Tapescript for Listening Tasks 2B and 2C — *Page 148*

THIEN: Hi, José and Maria. What's going on? You guys look kind of sad.

JOSÉ: Yeah. Well, I'm just so depressed about my English. I feel like my English hasn't improved in the longest time. And just yesterday, this guy made fun of my accent and told me I should learn to speak English.

THIEN: Really? Everyone understands *your* English, José. The guy must have been crazy. Did you ask him how many languages *he* spoke?

MARIA: *That* guy just spoke *one* language — *rude* English.

JOSÉ: Yeah. Hey, Thien. Your English has really improved lately. I remember last year I could hardly understand you, and now it's so much better. So, what's your secret? Find a girlfriend who speaks perfect English?

THIEN: Me? Girlfriend? I don't have a girlfriend. No, no girlfriend here. Do you see a girlfriend here?

MARIA: OK, OK, no girlfriend, Thien. But what has helped your English?

THIEN: Well. Thanks for the compliment. I guess it, it *has* gotten better huh? Maybe it was joining the ISC. Yes, the ISC has really helped my English.

MARIA AND JOSÉ: What's the ISC?

THIEN: The International Students' club. You haven't heard of it?

JOSÉ: Well, yeah, I guess I have. But how did that help?

THIEN: It gave me opportunities to speak English and meet people.

JOSÉ: So when does the club meet?

THIEN: Every other week, and there are parties and activities, too. Why don't you come to the next meeting on Thursday?

JOSÉ: Tuesday?

THIEN: No, Thursday at 12 noon in the activities center. You come too, Maria.

MARIA: OK. Anything to help my English.

THIEN: Wow. It's already 5 o'clock. I have to go meet Thu.

JOSÉ: Thu? Thu? Thu who? Is Thu female? No girlfriend hm?

THIEN: José, you don't give up, do you? She's just a friend. OK?

JOSÉ: Yeah, a friend, right. Met her at the ISC?

THIEN: As a matter of fact, I did. Maybe you'll meet someone, too. See you Thursday, José, and you too, Maria.

MARIA: Bye, Thien.

JOSÉ: Bye, Thien, and have a real good time with Thu.

MEI: Are you looking for ways to improve your spoken English? Do you need opportunities to speak English? Join us at the International Students' Club. That's the ISC every other Thursday at the Students' Activity Center at noon. Meet new friends, and improve your English. See you there.

Answers for Listening Tasks 2B and 2C — *Page 148*

B. 1. The International Students' Club (ISC).

2. They say the guy only speaks one language, *rude* English.

3. It will probably give information about the club.

C. 4. The place and time of the club meetings.

5. You might make some friends of the opposite sex.

Tapescript for Listening Task 3A — *Page 148*

STUDENT ANNOUNCER: Do you ever wish you could speak English better so you could get a college degree and get ahead in a promising career? You can do something about it today! Your English problems could be a thing of the past, and a degree and career in the field of your dreams can be made available at Taylor College. Just listen to these recent graduates.

GRADUATE 1: After studying ESL at Taylor's language center, I got my degree in nursing. Now I have a job doing what I have always wanted to do. Taylor's evening and weekend classes made it possible for me to finish my degree while working part time.

GRADUATE 2: Three years ago I had problems with my English. Now I have finished my degree in Business and am ready to start my own catalogue business from my home. The ESL program thoroughly prepared me for the work I needed to do for my degree, and the Business professors at Taylor were working professionals who had firsthand knowledge of the current issues involved in starting your own business.

GRADUATE 3: After finishing the ESL classes at Taylor, I graduated with a degree in Cosmetology. Then I got a job through Taylor's job-search program. Taylor helped me through the whole process, from creating my **résumé** to sharpening my interviewing skills.

STUDENT ANNOUNCER: You could be one of these Taylor graduates, ready to begin the career of your dreams. Come in or call today for information about how to register for classes. Call 2-Taylor. That's the number *2* and the letters *T, A, Y, L, O, R.* Call today to change your tomorrow.

Answers for Listening Task 3A — *Page 148*

1. Taylor College.
2. Learn to speak better English; get ahead in one's career; get a college degree.
3. Taylor's evening and weekend classes.
4. Taylor's ESL program and the good instructors and practical teaching.
5. Taylor's job-search program.
6. Answers will vary.

▶ CHAPTER 10

Help with Vocabulary — *Page 154*

5	a.	a sudden, unexplained change in emotions	mood swing (n.)
10	b.	to watch or care for something or someone	keep an eye on (v., idiom)
9	c.	beginning or original	initial (adj.)
1	d.	to be responsible for giving a party or event	host (v.)
2	e.	a place to give out information, or to have privacy	booth (n.)
14	f.	to deal with or handle	cope (v.)
3	g.	to listen to others without their knowledge or consent	eavesdrop (v.)
4	h.	a situation that causes one to want or do something	tempting (adj.)
12	i.	to reconsider a decision or have doubts about it	have second thoughts (v., idiom)
8	j.	to suppose, to believe something is true when there is no proof	assume (v.)
15	k.	friendly or kind toward guests	hospitable (adj.)
11	l.	high and low points, good and bad times	ups and downs (n.)
13	m.	outside one's country	abroad (adv.)
7	n.	the desire to eat	appetite (n.)
6	o.	to be removed from sight	disappear (v.)

Tapescript for Pre-Listening Task A — *Page 156*

MRS. ADAMS: ( ) Hello, Ms. Hernández. This is Jan Adams, Eiko's homestay mom. ( ) Fine, thank you. ( ) Well, as a matter of fact, that is why I am calling. Things are going fine, really, it's just that I worry when she has a **mood swing.** Well, she seems to be doing fine, and then suddenly she will **disappear** into her room, and I think she has been crying. ( ) Well, you're right. She had a great time at that party, but later that night she got so quiet and didn't eat dinner. It seems she hardly eats at all sometimes. Her lack of **appetite** really worries me. ( ) No. There aren't, really. I guess I shouldn't be so anxious about it then. You think it is normal that she cries at times? ( ) Thank you. That makes me feel better, but don't tell her I called you. Well, thank you, Ms. Hernández. ( ) OK, and thanks again. ( ) Bye.

Tapescript for Listening Task A — *Page 156*

MS. HERNÁNDEZ: Patty Hernández speaking. How can I help you?

MRS. ADAMS: Hello, Ms. Hernández. This is Jan Adams, Eiko's homestay mom.

MS. HERNÁNDEZ: Yes, of course, Mrs. Adams. How are you?

MRS. ADAMS: Fine, thank you.

MS. HERNÁNDEZ: And how are things going with Eiko? Is everything all right?

MRS. ADAMS: Well, as a matter of fact, that is why I am calling. Things are going fine, really, it's just that I worry when she has a mood swing.

MS. HERNÁNDEZ: Oh. Tell me about what has been happening.

MRS. ADAMS: Well, she seems to be doing fine, and then suddenly she will disappear into her room, and I think she has been crying.

MS. HERNÁNDEZ: Really? I saw her at the International Students' Club party last weekend, and she seemed to be having a good time. I had to **assume** that she was adjusting.

MRS. ADAMS: Well, you're right. She had a great time at that party, but later that night she got so quiet and didn't eat dinner. It seems she hardly eats at all sometimes. Her lack of appetite really worries me.

MS. HERNÁNDEZ: The crying and loss in appetite are common in the **initial** stages of adjusting to another culture, but **keep an eye on** her, and see that things don't get worse. I know she is doing well in school. Are there any other things she does that worry you?

MRS. ADAMS: No. There aren't, really. I guess I shouldn't be so anxious about it then. You think it is normal that she cries at times?

MS. HERNÁNDEZ: Yes. She is probably homesick and could use some encouragement. Let her know you care and are available to talk. Remind her that emotional **ups and downs** are just part of the acculturation process. I'll make a point to see her this week to learn whether she wants to talk about anything that is bothering her.

MRS. ADAMS:	Thank you. That makes me feel better, but don't tell her I called you.
MS. HERNÁNDEZ:	I won't, and I'm sure Eiko will be fine. It's good to know you are concerned and keeping an eye on her.
MRS. ADAMS:	Well, thank you, Ms. Hernández.
MS. HERNÁNDEZ:	I'll get in touch with you after I speak with her if I sense anything is wrong.
MRS. ADAMS:	OK, and thanks again.
MS. HERNÁNDEZ:	You are more than welcome, Mrs. Adams. Bye.
MRS. ADAMS:	Bye.

Answers for Listening Task A — *Page 156*

1. Mrs. Adams is concerned about Eiko's mood swings.
2. Ms. Hernández had seen Eiko having a good time at the ICS party.
3. Going to her room, crying, and lack of appetite.
4. Encourage Eiko, let her know that you'll talk, and understand the difficulties of cultural adjustment.

Tapescript and Answers for Pre-Speaking Task 2A — *Page 160* (*Answers are underlined.*)

MEI:	I'm going to explain the steps that you take to celebrate Chinese New Year. Have you heard about Chinese New Year?
MAGDA:	Mmm—maybe. The last day of the year with a dragon dance and firecrackers.
MEI:	Yes, but Chinese New Year takes place in January or February. It's different every…. it is based on the lunar calendar, so it's on a different day every year.
MAGDA:	What was that word? Lunar? What does that mean?
MEI:	Lunar means moon. The calendar based on the moon.
MAGDA:	Oh, I get it. OK, go on.
MEI:	So, as I was saying, the first step is preparation. You prepare three things. The most important thing you prepare is food. Some examples of food that you prepare are fish and seaweed. A fish dish is very important because fish in Chinese has the same sound as the word abundance. "Yu" means fish in Chinese, and abundance has the same sound.

MAGDA: Abundance? What does abundance mean?

MEI: Like more than enough. More than enough food, money, children, happiness.

MAGDA: Like extra, <u>right</u>?

MEI: Exactly. Seaweed is the same because it has the same sound as prosperity. You know what I mean by prosperity?

MAGDA: To be rich, not poor.

MEI: <u>Uh-HUH.</u> The second thing you prepare is the envelopes for the lucky money. You get bright red paper and wrap up money to give to the children.

MAGDA: Only children get the money?

MEI: Yes. Anyone who is married gives lucky money to all the relatives who are children. OK. So, the last thing to prepare is the new clothing. Everyone wears new clothing on New Year's so you have to either sew or buy the new clothing.

MAGDA: <u>Let me see if I understand correctly.</u> The first step is preparation, and the three things to prepare are food, especially fish and seaweed, for they symbolize abundance and prosperity; the red envelopes for the lucky money; and finally the new clothes.

MEI: <u>Mmm-HMMM.</u> That covers it. The next step is New Year's Eve itself. On that night you get together with all the relatives and eat all the food that you prepared. That is called the closing-the-year feast. You close the old year. Everyone is really happy, especially the children, for they get to wear new clothes and even gold chains, and they get the red envelopes with money. The next day you could have a dragon dance and set off firecrackers, too, as you said at the beginning.

MAGDA: How much money is in the envelopes?

MEI: <u>Well, let me think. Mmmm….</u> It depends, I guess, on how much the family can give. It is not really important how much you give; like just $2 or $20 is fine. It has to be an even number. It gives good luck to both you, the giver, and the kids who get the money. So, the last step is opening the new year, and that is celebrated with a feast, too. It is important to visit all the relatives. You need to go to the oldest relatives first, to show respect. So, that's about it. <u>Would you like me to clarify anything?</u>

MAGDA: When exactly does the opening feast happen? The next day?

MEI: <u>Well. How can I put it?</u> It is not really set. It has to be an even day from New Year's, like six days. Chinese are very superstitious.

MAGDA: You mean they believe in ghosts and stuff?

MEI: <u>What I'm trying to say is</u> they believe that things you do or don't do will cause you good or bad luck. You know, like breaking a mirror will be bad luck, but getting money will bring you good luck, especially on New Year's.

MAGDA: Let's see, now. There are three steps to Chinese New Year: the preparation, the actual New Year's Eve feast that closes the year, and the next meal that opens the year.

MEI: <u>What else?</u>

MAGDA: The preparations include preparing the food, like fish and seaweed; preparing the lucky money in red envelopes, which can be like $2 or $20; and then getting new clothes.

MEI: And jewelry sometimes, like gold chains.

MAGDA: Oh, yeah, the gold chains. The next step is New Year's Eve, when you eat and give out the money. And finally, like six days later, you eat again to open the new year with the relatives. <u>Right?</u>

MEI: Yes. That was really good.

Answers for Post-Speaking Task 2B — *Page 163*

1. fear
2. superiority
3. hatred
4. curiosity
5. tolerance
6. acceptance

▶ VOCABULARY REVIEW

Answers for Chapters 6 to 10 — *Pages 171–180*

Chapter 6: *Chicken-Out Charlie*

1. cannot stand,   2. enormous,   3. fondest,   4. stand out,   5. lottery,
6. impromptu,   7. stressed out,   8. confident,   9. slip,   10. motivation,
11. adjacent,   12. or else

Chapter 7: *"Washington, Here We Come!"*

1. persuade,   2. allot,   3. controversial,   4. proposition,   5. anecdote,
6. relevant,   7. biased,   8. deterrent,   9. refute,   10. inaccurate,
11. rapport   12. stand in awe

Chapter 8: Life or Death?

1. versus, 2. fetus, 3. sacrifice, 4. euthanasia, 5. cross-examine,
6. contribute, 7. mandatory, 8. inmate, 9. abolish, 10. offensive,
11. defensive, 12. censorship, 13. construct

Chapter 9: A Recipe for a Résumé

1. potluck, 2. samosa, 3. put off, 4. prop, 5. lift, 6. résumé,
7. attain, 8. keep on the lookout for, 9. brainstorm, 10. eliminate,
11. inadequacy, 12. mention

Chapter 10: Gossip from the Girls' Room

1. eavesdrop, 2. tempting, 3. booth, 4. mood swing, 5. host,
6. assumed, 7. abroad, 8. cope, 9. disappear, 10. keep an eye on,
11. hospitable, 12. appetite, 13. ups and downs, 14. initial,
15. have second thoughts